SINGAPORE CONTEMPORARY ARTISTS SERIES
VINCENT LEOW

This book is published in conjunction with the Tags & Treats: Works by Vincent Leow exhibition at the Singapore Art Museum between 6 August and 17 October 2010.

Photo credits: All images in this book courtesy of Vincent Leow and the Singapore Art Museum.

Please direct all enquiries to the Publisher:
Singapore Art Museum
71 Bras Basah Road
Singapore 189555
www.singaporeartmuseum.sg

Curator
David Chew

Research Assistant
Naomi Wang

Designed and produced by:
Editions Didier Millet
121 Telok Ayer Street #03-01
Singapore 068590

Printed in Singapore by **SC (Sang Choy) International Pte Ltd**

The opinions expressed in this publication are solely the writers' and not the Publisher's.

ISBN
978-981-4260-41-1

page 4: *White Portrait*, 2009, oil on canvas, 100 x 80 cm, artist collection
page 80: *Conversations with a Femur Bone* (detail of an installation), 2010, mixed media, artist collection

SINGAPORE CONTEMPORARY ARTISTS SERIES
VINCENT LEOW

sam
singapore**art**museum

CONTENTS

Money Suit (installation detail), 1992, mixed media,
Singapore Art Museum collection

FOREWORD

The challenge and reality of contemporary art entered the Singaporean public imagination from the late 1980s, following the emergence of a generation of artists associated with pioneering collectives such as The Artist Village and 5th Passage. More than two decades later, the issues and questions surrounding this intense, complex and emotional period in our art history has started to generate a lot of interest, especially seen against the backdrop of the recent surge of market interest in contemporary art. Vincent Leow is one such artist whose artistic career is linked to this period in Singapore's art history, and who has also continued to develop in response to changing realities. Years of being an educator at art schools, like the LASALLE College of the Arts and recently the Sharjah College of Art and Design (UAE), has sensitised him to look at not only how audiences react but how they can better appreciate contemporary art.

As the institution focusing on contemporary Southeast Asian art, the Singapore Art Museum (SAM) is celebrating this rich artistic scene created by artists like Leow and his peers, through a series of mid-career exhibitions and books on each individual artist's career and practice. SAM hopes that such initiatives will help foster greater dialogue and engagement with the artistic community and our public.

I would like to thank Vincent and his wife Yvonne for their involvement in this exhibition, as well as Vincent's patrons and supporters who have assisted in one way or another to make this exhibition and publication a success.

Tan Boon Hui
Director
Singapore Art Museum

An Elegiac Rebellion

David Chew

Introduction

Vincent Leow's earliest memory as a child was of being intrigued at age four or five by his ability to create objects and art, making toy guns, daggers and swords from leftover pieces of wood he found around him.

"Where I was growing up, my neighbour was a wood craftsman. Even as a child, his tools and skills fascinated me – how he transformed a plain looking chair or wooden chest by his skills with amazing Chinese landscapes, dragons and patterns." (Interview with Vincent Leow, 2009)

Although Vincent had always received below average grades in art class in school, he nevertheless felt that this was separate from the level of creativity a person possessed. At

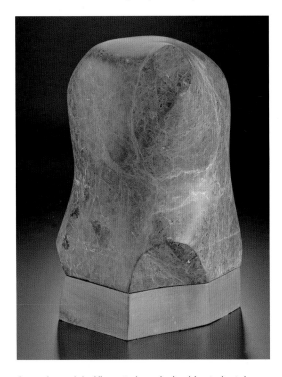

An early work by Vincent, done during his student days. *Torso*, undated, marble and wood, 30.2 x 20.5 x 27.8 cm, Singapore Art Museum collection

this young age, it sowed in him the seed of determination to pursue "being creative" in the non-traditional sense of being an artist.

Having a keen interest in architecture and design, Vincent translated this creative energy into becoming an architecture draughtsman after serving his National Service stint, and later joined a landscape design company. It was during this period, when he was working with creative colleagues, that Vincent decided it was time to take the plunge. He enrolled at the new St Patrick's Art Centre (now known as the LASALLE College of the Arts), which was founded in 1984 by Brother Joseph McNally.

While his introductory classes laid the foundation to the different art media, it was sculpture-making that interested Vincent the most, rekindling the idea of making and producing something solid from ideas and concepts. His first art school project was, not surprisingly, woodcarving. Vincent continued exploring (in addition to the requisite drawing and painting courses) marble-carving as well as metal-welding throughout his first formal arts course.

Born in 1961, amidst the throes of Singapore's pre and post-independence era, Vincent grew up during a dramatic period of political and social change. In a mere two decades, rapid modernisation as well as nationalism was taking root against a backdrop of transnational economics and global commodity diversification. When Vincent finished his foundational arts education at LASALLE in the mid-1980s, he would emerge into a highly charged environment and milieu, in which the Singapore art scene was undergoing a seismic shift (Storer, 2007, p. 12).

The Flowering of the Contemporary

Vincent occupies a significant place in the development of contemporary art in Singapore. His prolific art practice has always been rooted in debates over contemporary Singapore identity.

Alongside fellow contemporary artists such as Cheo Chai Hiang, Tang Da Wu and Amanda Heng, Vincent is part of the group of artists in the 1970s and 1980s who began to focus on the idea and concept behind an artwork, rather than simply the execution i.e., the speculation behind a work, rather than the rendering of actual appearances.

These new frontiers of visual art in Singapore were pioneered in the 1970s by young artists then, such as Cheo and Tang who started to challenge the traditional definitions of art where "beautiful pictures" had been produced, and the primary definition of art had been limited to the medium of painting (Sabapathy & Briggs, 2000, p. 17).

What these young artists proposed was not just a change in aesthetics and style, but an ideological shift from the need to create sacrosanct artworks that were imprisoned by conventional and outmoded aesthetics, to the propagation of the tenets of conceptual art, such as the focus on ideas, concepts and processes, and adopting engaged attitudes towards the everyday world as a resource for materials, subject-matter and methods of making (Sabapathy & Briggs, 2000, p. 27). What this meant for the Singapore art scene was an opening up and expansion of stylistic possibilities in ways to create art, engender the birth of pluralism, and refocus the purpose and meaning of art production and consumption.

Members of The Artists Village: Vincent is seated third from the right.

Numerous scholars and writers have observed the pluralisation of the cultural climate of the 1980s, brought about by the forces of modernisation that created disruptive conditions which ironically facilitated the emergence of new art movements and artistic possibilities, spurring younger artists to engage in critical self-questioning and new forms of expression.

The attempt to negotiate these conflicts and disputes of differences in society manifested itself in a form of creative rebelliousness, which William Lim in his book *Alternate (Post) Modernity* defines as "fuzzy logic and spaces of indeterminacy, relaxing the gates of reason in order to allow certain processes of evolving alternate traditions" (Lim, 2003, p. 17–18).

Coupled with the socio-political conditions of the two preceding decades of rapid nation-building in the 1960s and 1970s, the 1980s witnessed a flowering of experimental stylistic forms that expanded the field beyond painting and sculpture to installation and performance art, as well as experimental theatre. Responses to this resulted in numerous artist-organised activities, which included the formation of groups and movements such as The Necessary Stage, the Trimurti group of artists, as well as The Artists Village (TAV) (Storer, 2007, p. 12).

In 1988, two key events took place in the development of contemporary visual arts. One was the Trimurti exhibition held at the Goethe-Institut, featuring the artists S. Chandrasekaran, Goh Ee Choo and Salleh Japar. Focusing on the Hindu concept of Trimurti, which is the drawing together of creation, preservation and dissolution into a single, united force, the exhibition combined Asian traditions with modern sensibilities and perspectives through a variety of media to create a new artistic language (Storer, 2007, p. 12–13).

The other key event of the year was the establishment of TAV, led by artists who were inspired by Western art movements such as conceptual art and the Fluxus movement. In response to an increasingly urbanised Singapore, TAV was set up in one of the few remaining rural areas in Singapore, in Lorong Gambas (Ulu Sembawang), as an open-studio environment that enabled experimentation and discussion. At its peak, it had some 35 artists living and working on the site, and another 50 participating in exhibitions held there.

Initiated by Tang and several other artists, the collective and its open-studio environment (a vehement response against the commercial gallery system) soon became a "hothouse for creativity". Creating a communal environment for artists to interact and collaborate, it encouraged process-based studio situations, and allowed artists to explore new forms and

ideas, as well as open up interactivity with audiences – the rise of what Sabapathy terms a "kinship between audiences and the artwork" (Storer, 2007, p. 13 & Sabapathy, 2000, p. 11).

Vincent, as well as other young artists such as Wong Shih Yaw, Amanda Heng, Tang Mun Kit, Koh Nguang How and Lee Wen, came to be associated with TAV, and their works were influenced by the contemporary interdisciplinary practices as well as conceptual focus that was part of the TAV movement (Sabapathy, 2000, p. 15). Vincent, commenting on the period, noted that it was akin to rediscovering art all over again.

Cut Throat, 1989, oil on canvas,
100 x 130 cm, artist collection

Initially attached to sculptor Han Sai Poh, Vincent found traditional carving limiting due to its slowness in expressing artistic ideas, and his experience at TAV made him realise that performance art and painting were more immediate and spontaneous.

Works such as *Lucky Strike*, *Yellow Circle*, *Cut Throat* and *Two Men* (all done in 1989) express a gestural and spontaneous quality. Together with the strong colours, unruly brushstrokes as well as the violent subject matter of the paintings, Vincent's works from this period are highly charged with strong emotion and anger, challenging the hitherto subdued temperament of painting in Singapore. Collectively, they also contain "a rogue element in painting", rebelling against the local dominant modes and styles of the time, which were lyrical and formalistic abstraction or realist and naturalistic styles (Poh, 2007, p. 14).

These newer forms of art, Vincent notes, were more flexible in conveying ideas, like how performance art uses the body and installation art uses space, respectively, as canvases for expression. Vincent came to realise that an artist's idea and his visual expression should not be limited by discipline. This expressive quality in his works would continue to reveal itself throughout his career, from performance art and later to paintings.

"I wanted to challenge different things, I wanted to challenge pretty art, I wanted an alternative to that, and as a young artist I wanted to push the boundaries, to challenge safe art such as Anthony Poon, and not just the style, but also subject matter in art," says Vincent on this period of his work. (Interview with Vincent Leow, 2009)

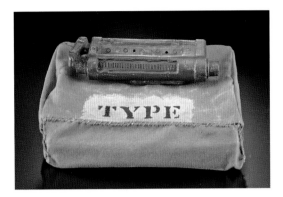

Type, 1990, plastic, canvas and bronze, 12.5 x 25.5 x 20.0 cm, Singapore Art Museum collection

Birth of a Satirist: The American Days

At the age of 28, fresh from his brief time at TAV, Vincent decided to further his artistic skills, spending three years at the Maryland Institute College of Art in Baltimore to pursue his Masters of Fine Arts from 1989 to 1991.

Certainly, the exposure to artists like Cheo and Tang would have influenced Vincent's decision to further his fine arts study. Both had benefited from an overseas education which emphasised cross-disciplinary practices, as well as a de-emphasis on prescription and instruction in favour of processes of thinking and devising (Sabapathy & Briggs, 2000, p. 21–22). Vincent had hoped to explore this within the structural confines of a systematic study of the fine arts, but his choice of school and country to do this was significant and telling of the direction his practice would take after his studies.

Unlike Cheo and Tang who went to the UK, Vincent attended one of the oldest art colleges in the United States, the Maryland Institute College of Art, which boasted an alumni that included composer John Cage, master printer Ken Tyler and painter Elaine de Kooning.

Vincent (standing on right) with his lecturer (standing on left) American artist Salavatore Scarpitta, in Baltimore (1919–2007)

Certainly, the college's emphasis on technique and foundation was one attraction for Vincent, allowing him to explore in more detail the act and art of painting.

Works from this period were of single objects, reminiscent of the still-life tradition in classical painting, but Vincent explored the material and texture of paints as well as the canvas itself, questioning the very definition of painting.

He notes how he spent one semester drawing furiously in numerous sketchbooks, "just to push out the ideas on what exactly is painting," he says. "I wanted to go back to painting, to discover and think more about what could be considered art, it was about turning the banal and everyday into art". (Interview with Vincent Leow, 2009)

Vincent's paintings shifted its focus towards building up density, texture and scale. *Yellow Field* (1990), for example, with its monumental scale has the rich textural surface of classical landscape, but Vincent's painting explores stretching an everyday object, a T-shirt, into a

landscape painting of a runway. Others such as *Milk* (1989), *Shield The Lamp* (1990) are still-life studies of a single object. *Buoy* (1990), which characteristically fulfils Vincent's wish that his artworks take on a life of their own after he is done with them, has an added dimension to its intent of exploring texture and the painting surface. Wasps had chosen to build their nest right on the canvas, above the centre of the buoy itself, adding a third dimension to the surface of the artwork.

But the country too, was in itself interesting in relation to Vincent's practice, as his works during this period when he was in the US attest. The 1980s and early 1990s, after all, was the period in which capitalism was back in fashion, when the financial world and the stock market were glamourised in the mass media, with the celebration of icons such as Donald Trump, and the making of movies such as *Wall Street* (1987).

Vincent's interest in current affairs, in particular, manifested itself in works such as

Fishabunga (1990), which commented on both the ready-made (the work itself is painted on a found roof awning canvas) and the culture of mass production in society; *Dumbo* (1990) which commented on the role of mass media such as television in our lives; and later on, *Red & White* (2000) are layered with polka dots to represent the pixelated screen we view the world through on TV screens. Vincent's new visual language played on the advertising culture of sending messages out repeatedly, not unlike propaganda, so people remember it (which Vincent would appropriate to establish his own social statements).

Vincent commented on the heady dominance of commercialisation in the US by recasting James Brown as American President in the US dollar bill, and recasting the painting of the Last Supper on a Pizza Hut tablecloth. *Dumbo* and *Aladdin & Genie* (1994) were commentaries on politics – both the rabbits and the elephant

Mountian Cow Milk Factory, 1998,
mixed media installation, private collections

were used by Vincent to represent political parties. This refined and developed voice of social commentary was a distinct contrast to his earlier raw, gestural paintings.

Vincent's use of this new visual language and tone created a new voice for himself, a mischievous tone beneath the more formal qualities of art, together with more serious messages and social statements.

Even after he returned to Singapore in 1992, globalisation and the homogenisation of culture and images, as well as technology such as cloning, became the focus of Vincent's work as he engaged with contemporary Southeast Asian urban life and consumerism, as well as questioning Singaporean social and cultural values.

A 1994 painting entitled *Golden Goose* looks like a gigantic label for a food product, at the centre of which is a golden goose with golden eggs labelled "quality Singapore eggs", inspired by a comment by the then Prime Minister Goh Chok Tong on being careful not to kill the goose that lays the golden eggs, implying Singaporeans had to still run on the treadmill of economic development (Wee, 2001, p. 7).

Vincent continued this playful engagement and establishment of social statements with his famous *Mountian Cow Factory* series (1998). The title of this series of works were deliberately misspelled, and made in multiples, they were also a comment on the major breakthrough in science of the time, the cloning of Dolly the Sheep. The series had a Warholian quality, with vibrant bright colours, and like Warhol, Vincent produced multiple versions, altering only the background colours. This series of multiple cow paintings were paired with life-sized sculptures of cows that were placed in public places.

A Space (and Time) for Performance Art

Vincent's homecoming to Singapore in 1992 also found him returning to performance art.

While Vincent downplays the significance of his performance-art pieces within his body of work – noting that it really was just a few performance pieces he had done then – even he cannot discount the monumental impact of his performances on the relatively young contemporary art scene in Singapore. Vincent admits it took a life of its own.

And it's not hard to see why.

The very qualities of performance art – its focus on the process, its very transient and ephemeral nature, and its potential for establishing and promoting a kinship between audiences and artists, seeks to alter the traditional one-sided relationship of audiences as consumers of art (Sabapathy & Briggs, 2000, p. 27). By also taking art out of safe constructs, performance art more often than not shocks audiences into reassessing their own definitions and notions of art.

Against the context and background of an enforced normality that belies the socialisation experience in Singapore, performance art (till today) exists in an alternative and liminal space, despite having the ability to relate immediately to our environment and to express a sort of angst.

Apart from TAV, groups like 5th Passage had also formed during the time Vincent was studying abroad. Founded in 1991, the group managed an artist collective gallery in what was lauded as the first corporate-sponsored space in a commercial shopping mall. Run by artists such as Suzann Victor, Susie Lingham and Iris Tan, the group focused both on a

Lifestyles of the Rich and Famous, 1992, **Hong Bee Warehouse**

professional and structured way of art production, as well as issues of gender and identity, primarily concentrating on alternative art, such as performance.

Vincent's return from the US saw him exploring the spontaneous quality of performance art, raising issues related to capitalism and the commoditisation of art through performances such as *Lifestyles of the Rich and Famous: The Three-Legged Toad* (1992) and *Coffee Talk* (1993).

Lifestyles playfully took digs at the capitalist complicities of arts and culture. It involved Vincent performing in a suit, shoes and Daddy Warbucks hat, all fabricated from fake US dollar bills in large denominations.

Coffee Talk was done as an installation mimicking a café setting, in which, after briefly addressing the audience about issues related to the arts, Vincent urinated into a coffee cup and drank it. He went on to cut bits of his hair that he placed into envelopes addressed to prominent people in the Singapore arts scene. He subsequently bottled his urine as "limited editions" and sold them to art collectors. (Nadarajan, 2007, p. 90)

"The performance for Coffee Talk, *of drinking my own urine, came from the initial idea of consuming my own by-product, and it was about being in the art myself, of including myself in the artwork, as well as the dialogue exchanges and reactions from the process of performing that work. Bottling my urine after the performance as documentation, but also selling it as limited edition pieces of artwork, was about the commoditisation of my by-product, and how the artwork could take on a life of its own six months after the performance itself, yet still forming a relationship with the society it is at that moment in time."* (Interview with Vincent Leow, 2009)

Today, bottles of *The Artist's Urine* and the *Money Suit* are still as instantly identified with these past performances, and are a constant reminder of Vincent's skills in negotiating between commerce and the art world.[1]

Brief as it was, the performance-art period in Vincent's artistic career is significant in representing the alternative nature of his practice, as well as its ability to go beyond merely exploring visual languages and to be critical and rebelling against the mainstream.

To Vincent, this period of his practice was part of ongoing explorations on the possibilities for interaction with audiences. "The question is: how important that audience response is, and how strong the reaction," he surmises.

From Satire to Alter Ego

The return to Singapore, and its hybridity and pastiche of cultures, led Vincent to start what would be a significant shift in his artistic career – turning to mythology as one of his conceptual devices to explore the notion of identity as a Singaporean, in Southeast Asia and the globalised world.

Singapore, after all, created a shared history and identity post-1965, the very symbol of which could be said to be captured by the kitsch animal emblem known as the Merlion[2] – a construct of the Singapore Tourism Board in 1964.

The use of animals in Vincent's art can be seen in his Andy series, featuring a half-man, half-dog creature that has featured prominently in his work until today. The notion of the half-man, half-animal was an idea that Vincent had explored even in his TAV days. Used as an alter ego, Vincent's development of the Andy image was a natural evolvement in his use of animals as symbols in his work.

Bombs Away, 1996, oil on canvas, 120 x 150 cm, private collection

Hawk, 2006, stainless steel (edition of 5), 240 x 150 x 150 cm, Singapore Art Museum collection

Based on real life pets he kept, such as his rabbits Aladdin and Genie, his rooster Hawk (which became an Andy sculpture nicknamed Hawk after the pet rooster), Vincent intentionally uses domestic animals to create a contemporary urban mythology – with a clear blurring of lines between reality and fiction in his work over time. The reincarnation of Andy in his art, while inspired by his pet dog Andy, takes on an uncanny resemblance to Vincent himself with each passing work.

Inspired by a postcard of Andy Warhol from which Vincent named his pet dog in Warhol's honour, the Andy series of narratives developed Vincent's satirical voice into a burlesque style that placed "Andy" in different situations and bodies. These paintings were colourful, bright, almost fairytale-like, evoking the sense of a creation of a mythical and magical setting. For instance, the very vibrant *Andy's Addiction* (1996) shows Andy against a candy-red background that looks almost good to eat, or the mischievous *Bombs Away* (1996) that had Andy naughtily defecating bombs on an otherwise sunny day.

Vincent started creating a series of work that could communicate and generate a narrative about the mixing and breeding of different cultures. Taking inspiration from traditional legends and stories of mythical creatures from various cultures such as the Sphinx, Phoenix and Monkey God, the aim was to create an urban contemporary mythical but fictional character that would share characteristics of being both human and animal.

These creatures have been written about previously as hybrids: i.e. part human, part animal, part monster. They would help Vincent define his identity as an Asian artist with Western art training, as well as a person living in a country with both Eastern and Western ideologies mixing together. In essence, the artist was toying with the idea of hybridisation as a form of mongrelisation through this alter-ego Andy. Beyond simple hybridity, this was also a means of forgetting and erasing the past through the creation of a new set of myths and stories.

Andy would reappear with characteristic anarchy in Vincent's paintings throughout his subsequent career, grinning from within the sacred, sanctified compositions of classical and iconic masterpieces, such as in the Renaissance Andy series. Vincent intentionally "cross-breeds" (and in doing so ignoring the rules of) high and low art sources, allowing the creatures to pop out into real life in the form of life-sized sculptures. This series of work would feature most significantly in the 2007 Singapore Season exhibition Andy's Pranks & Swimming Lessons, and the 2007 Singapore Pavilion at the 52nd Venice Biennale. The sculptures, *Andy's Pranks*,

Hawk, and *Andy's Wonderland* (all 2006) are literally polished life-like representations of Andy, begetting a seductive idol-like worship of these kitschy figures set in a different reality.

The success and popularity of the Andy series lies in its exploration of issues at the very heart of the Singapore identity, leading to the questioning of self in relation to both ongoing socio-political situations and where we come from, and doing so using contemporary art as a platform to discuss mainstream culture and issues.

On Identity, Legacy and Death: Back to Painting and Classical Art

In a strange twist of events, Vincent's pet dog Andy, on which the series of works were based on, passed away in 2009 at the age of 14, at which point the series takes on an even more poignant and commemorative significance.

Vincent's latest works are less "in-your-face", more subdued and quieter in spirit. The *Conversations with a Femur Bone* installation, created based on life-sized human femur bones, suggests the baggage of memories that death leaves behind for the living – heavy and unwieldy – yet still injecting Vincent's trademark playfulness, conjuring up the ghost of the half-man half-dog Andy, who would view bones more as a treat.

Blacked-out portraits (*Portrait and Hand*, *Hawk Portrait* and *Salam*, all 2009) that are paired with the above installation seemingly retreat from the creation of another identity (re: the Andy series), to the erasing of it – a stripping away of representation. All that is left are traces of the person through their hands. Contrasted against the colourful backgrounds,

these portraits hark back to the classical painting tradition of portraits of the elite, but are also inspired by the *momento mori* (remember you will die) genre of classical paintings that remind mankind of mortality, and the futility of vanities. In Vincent's case, he inverts the very nature of portraiture painting to question that very vanity – how do you still show representation without showing it.

"The idea of black is not just about death, but it is also of one's identity being anonymous, yet catching glimpses of a person. What do we look for or how do we judge something, if it is all blacked out?" (Interview with Vincent Leow, 2009)

One of the works, *Portrait & Veil* (2009), resembles da Vinci's famous *Mona Lisa* – only the portrait of Lisa Gherardini is missing, the very subject it is meant to celebrate. The solid black human silhouettes tempt one to impose and project one's own memories onto a life remembered, suggesting an elusive quality that a painting surface can never fully capture.

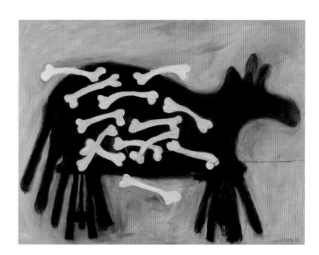

Animal Bones, 2010, oil on canvas, 72 x 100 cm, artist collection

Going back to the classical genre of portrait painting, is a certain "death", says Vincent. It is the only way to start afresh.

The idea of death and its association with the colour black, is Vincent's recalibration of his role as an artist and where his new direction will take him. The old must die for the new to be reborn, to start from ground zero and go back to neutral.

His other two new installations, *Feet Remembered* and *Heads Remembered* (both 2010), commemorate the lives of the common people. The trishaw drivers who pound the streets of Yogyakarta (a work Vincent had done previously during a two-month residency in Yogyakarta at the Cemeti Art Foundation in 2000), are commemorated through the work *Feet Remembered*, where clay casts of their feet are celebrated on monumental plinths normally reserved for national heroes.

Heads Remembered is an installation of ceramic busts of an unknown person, lacking specific facial details, in a cemetery or state-park that pays the same homage to unsung lives of the everyman. Similar to the way his Andy series celebrated the life of his pet mongrel, Vincent champions the importance of every single life lived, no matter how seemingly insignificant.

For Vincent, these more metaphorical and abstract works – a clear shift from the figurative – are part of the development of his ideas of playing with fiction and the fantastical, working with the everyday and banal to create a story. At the same time, he adds an element of unresolved discomfort for audiences viewing his art that they not only project their own meanings to his work, but also find their own resolution.

Sunflower, 2009, oil on canvas, 100 x 80 cm, artist collection

Epilogue

Originating from Vincent's TAV days, in which he was part of a collective which encouraged direct audience engagement that reflected and commented on everyday life in Singapore, the idea of challenging how the general public views and appreciates art is a common thread that runs through his work.

It is this audience reaction and response to art that still intrigues Vincent. He continues to explore the idea of how the framing and context of exhibiting artwork contribute to people's consumption of an artist's works.

But even so, "the artist," says Vincent, "only contributes to the artwork at the beginning of its life. After its creation, the life of the artwork develops much further even after the artist is done with it."

Endnotes

1. Other performance-art pieces Vincent did during this period was *1000 Ways To Cross a Plank*, about negotiating space and reacting to space and real time, which Vincent felt was the real potential of performance (at that time).
2. Designed as an emblem to denote the rediscovery of Singapura as recorded in the *Malay Annals*, the half-lion, half-fish figure aptly captures Singapore's hybrid nature of an Asian nation with Western ideals. The Merlion, however, has no basis in Singapore's history or culture, and is a construct of the Singapore Tourism Board.

Bibliography

Kwok Kian Chow, *Channels & Confluences: A History of Singapore Art*, Singapore Art Museum, Singapore, 1996.

Kwok Kian Woon, *The Artists Village 20 Years On: Locating & Positioning The Artists Village in Singapore and Beyond*, Singapore Art Museum and The Artists Village, Singapore, 2009.

Lim, William, *Alternate (Post) Modernity: An Asian Perspective*, Select Publishing, Singapore, 2003.

Lim, William, *Asian Alterity*, Mainland Press, Singapore, 2008.

Leow, Vincent, Personal interview with Artist, Dec 2009.

Nadarajan, Gunanlan, *Contemporary Art in Singapore: Vincent Leow*, Institute of Contemporary Arts Singapore, Singapore, 2007.

Poh, Lindy, *Andy's Pranks & Swimming Lessons*, Soobin Art Int'l, Xin Beijing Gallery, Singapore and Beijing, 2007.

Sabapathy, T.K., *Many In One: 25 Years of Art From Singapore*, National Museum of Singapore, Singapore, 1991.

Sabapathy, T.K., *Sculpture in Singapore*, National Museum of Singapore, Singapore, 1991.

Sabapathy, T.K., *Cheo Chai-Hiang: The Thirty-Six Strategies*, Casula Powerhouse Arts Centre, NSW, Australia, 2000.

Sabapathy, T.K. & C. Briggs, *Cheo Chai-Hiang: Thoughts And Processes (Rethinking The Singapore River)*, Nanyang Academy of Fine Arts & Singapore Art Museum, Singapore, 2000.

Storer, Russell, *Contemporary Art in Singapore: Making Space: Historical Contexts of Contemporary Art in Singapore*, Institute of Contemporary Arts Singapore, Singapore, 2007.

Wee, C.J.W.-L., Four Eyes, Cloudy Skies: Vincent Leow, *The Ongoing Process of 'Making' Art*, Singapore: Atelier Frank & Lee, Singapore, 2001.

Interview with the Artist

The following is based on an interview with the artist, Vincent Leow, conducted by Tan Boon Hui, Director of the Singapore Art Museum, on 28 June 2010.

TBH How long have you been teaching in Sharjah?

VL Two and a half years; it will be three years in Sharjah University, United Arab Emirates, when I return in September 2010.

TBH Let's start from the current day. In the two and a half years that you have been in Sharjah, how would you describe your thinking about art, and specifically, about the work you have done before Sharjah?

VL I left for Sharjah after participating in the Venice Biennale in 2007. Uprooting myself from Singapore to Sharjah has provided me with a different experience and perspective about my own work and art practice. Being in Sharjah has allowed me to re-examine my work in response to the tradition, culture and environment that I am now immersed in. In relationship to the place, I explore and research new subject matter as well as resources that I could introduce to my practice, to further develop my art.

TBH Comparing your experiences in Sharjah and when you first started out in Singapore, can you say a little bit more about Sharjah? What do you think is the concept and the purpose of art there, and what does it mean to be an artist in Sharjah? Why did Sharjah build all this infrastructure?

VL Art in Sharjah and in that region is still a challenging subject. The idea of figurative representation is usually debated in relation to tradition, culture and religion. However, only classes in the Fine Art and Medical faculties are conducted in English, everything else is in Arabic. This for me demonstrates that the country seeks to embrace and engage with contemporary art ideas and practices. The aim is also to become an important cultural destination through the building of world-class museums and performing centres, and events such as the Sharjah Biennale of Contemporary Art, the Dubai Art Fairs and the Abu Dhabi Art Fairs have been receiving attention.

TBH This cultural and artistic awakening must be very unusual in the context of Sharjah society. It is also very brave to suddenly have this.

VL Abu Dhabi, being the capital of the United Arab Emirates, has yet to have an art college that is fully dedicated to Fine Art Studies, but I do believe there will be one in the making soon. Sharjah, on the other hand, has not been on the same front as Abu Dhabi, which is

Desert Houses, 2009, oil on canvas, 20 x 40 cm, artist collection

considered the most cultural of all the UAE states, due to its efforts in the conservation and promotion of cultural heritage and the arts.

TBH Could you say a little more about your latest works using portraits and silhouette? There is a certain sort of paring down of the decorative or surface elements in your artworks.

VL I like the idea of how much one can present within a canvas or a work; how much a canvas should be filled with colours, detail and representations. One of my works titled *Salam*, for example, was shown at the Sharjah Art Museum. It depicts a local man with his hand close to his chest. Most of the local men are dressed in their traditional white *dishdash*. When the painting, basically an image of a silhouette, was exhibited, the local audiences referenced their tradition, culture and religion in their responses to the work. Some works which I did, inspired by motifs in Islamic architecture, with a mere suggestion of a cross or star provoked question. I was trying to eliminate as many details as possible; a little can be suggestive of a lot. I am glad the works have opened up different layers of reading and interpretation – which is interesting for me.

TBH In terms of stylistic development, what you are describing is quite interesting, sort of a classical idea in which an artist starts with basic means and techniques, and a certain style of aesthetics; and then the work gets more polished as the artist becomes more confident in the use of material; and these result in more elaborate and sophisticated work surfaces. Subsequently, the artist starts paring down; the emphasis is moved to small details, which can mean a lot.

VL I always feel that the subject matter is only a very small part of what the work presents. Instead, materials and texture can create the intensity in the work. Sometimes, how the materials are used by the artist can be actually much more interesting and satisfying for me.

TBH You are also thinking about the reception of the work and the different meanings they can have. These meanings can be triggered by small details, but they are meaningful in terms of the response from the viewer. If we take these, and look back at your earlier works, how do you compare your new works to the more provocative earlier works such as *Money Suit*, and your performance in which you drank your own urine?

VL I view all my past work and processes as very important phases in my career. Every piece of work, good or bad, leads to the next and they inform one another. If one looks at my past and current works,

Dome Landscape, 2009, oil on canvas, 20 x 40 cm, artist collection

in many ways there are also some links and connections in concepts, ideas, methods and materials. I view my past performances in terms of technique, method or material, and how these communicate an idea. Performance art as a medium was something I was not exposed to and I didn't learn at school, but I needed to find the vocabulary to execute the performance piece. I view my body as my "canvas" in a performance. The first solo performance art I did was based on an art performance by Joseph Beuys' *How To Explain Pictures To A Dead Hare* in which Beuys cradled a dead hare lovingly in his arms for three hours, walking it around and showing his drawings to the lifeless animal whilst explaining the paintings to it in an inaudible whisper. The hare symbolises birth for Beuys because it is born and burrows underground, later to emerge from the earth. Vaguely, I remember I painted myself white and used a slide projector to explain art to a found toy. I was attracted to the idea that performance art evokes immediate responses from the audience.

TBH Performance art for you was very much self-taught. It is interesting that despite this lack of formal knowledge during that period, performance art was flourishing.

VL Performance art was largely self-taught and I learnt "on the job". We (performance artists) looked at art books and images, but there were not many references for us, and I was fortunate that Tang Da Wu and his peers at that time contributed and provided valuable critiques, feedback and discussion.

TBH I'm thinking how, in another context, the contemporary Chinese artists learnt about Beuys and the Dada movement, for example, through photocopied texts. They started performance art in the East just like that.

VL Yes in that way it was similar. For example, I had to define my own parameters in performance art then. For instance, is there a time frame for the performance? Should there be a beginning and ending, and the use of props? How long is a performance supposed to be? Is it necessary for performance art to always be so long? I try to explore how I can combine performance art with my art knowledge, such as in *Money Suit*. After the performance, the prop turned into a sculpture. During the performance, I built a narrative for the piece and turned it into a sculpture as well as an installation. Similarly, in *The Artist's Urine*, I tried to sell my body's by-product, urine, and through this, the performance piece took on different dynamics of its own.

Milkweed, 2009, oil on canvas, 80 x 60 cm, artist collection

TBH You keep using the word "narrative". You say that there is narrative to your work, this is an old notion of art. Has that always been used in your work?

VL I do use narrative a lot because I would like my work to be able to communicate some story, whether real or fictional.

TBH You started off as a sculptor; how did you make the transition to painting?

VL I did sculpture at St. Patrick's. Back then, woodcarving was introduced to me when I did my foundation in Fine Art, and we were also taught other mediums of art such as drawing and painting, but I realised that I enjoyed the three-dimensional aspects of art the most. This was interesting, but I had so many ideas for my art that sculpture was just not immediate enough to express and capture my ideas. I had a renewed interest in painting during The Artists Village days [1988–1989], the period before I left for the US where I was exposed to the expressionistic style of painting. That made me even more interested in painting as I found my ideas could be executed faster; the expressionist style ran counter to the academic-realist style of painting as it created the possibility of capturing something very individualistic. When I did my Master, I focused on painting and mixed-media work.

TBH In your later paintings, you tend to focus on various series of motifs or images. What about the use of repetition of an image, what can you say about that in your work? Are you always intent on seizing upon one motif? For example, the cows in your *Mountian Cow Milk Factory* series?

VL It started out with the aluminum pieces *Big Head, Little People,* which came before *Mountian Cow Milk Factory.* The aluminum pieces in the former started first as a repetition, while the cow sculptures and paintings were inspired by the idea of cloning and making similar things. Cloning, Dolly the Sheep and the consumer society were the points of inspiration. I was also interested in the idea of propaganda from Chinese Cultural Revolution posters. I liked the idea of repetition; saying the same message (in slightly different forms) over and over again, and how these reminders make us remember. I also like the idea of interaction. When I did the installations for the paintings of *Mountian Cow Milk Factory,* I tried to put them in different public venues so that people started talking about them after seeing them so often.

Two Molehills, 2009, oil on canvas, 40 x 56 cm, artist collection

TBH I saw the prints you exhibited at Soo Bin's gallery in 2009, they look the same at first glance as they are all slightly different variants of essentially the same woodcut, but I began to see the individuality in each work after some time. But it requires hard work to do this.

VL I like the impact when similar works are put together, of being confronted with so many similar works. The works can be equally powerful without being very different from one other. I can be critical of them even though they are quite similar. Amongst the eight pieces of woodcut prints at Soo Bin's, for example, there was one which is my favourite. Imperfection is an interesting aspect of the artwork.

TBH You are right; there is a level in which the repetition relentlessly drills itself in, almost like propaganda.

VL Adopting the concept of repetition, for me, is an effective tool as this connects me with the various research that I am interested in. This concept and idea allows my works to be adapted to different sites and scales effectively.

TBH Using the same idea of repetition, can you tell me about your work leading up to the Venice Biennale? Why Andy?

VL The painting *Andy's Addiction* came from the idea of mythologies, and how people believe in deities that are half-human, half-animal – taking reference from Hindu Gods and Chinese mythology. I wanted to create something with a domestic animal – I used to own a rooster, two rabbits and dogs – for what would be a contemporary, urban mythology. When I was invited to the Venice Biennale, the idea I wanted was to transform something banal and unimportant into something important. I wanted to transform Andy's "status" from a domestic mongrel to be idolised as a god or deity.

Dog on Yellow, 2009, oil on canvas,
30 x 40 cm, artist collection

TBH What was the intention?

VL I wanted to make Andy look attractive. Like the way we are attracted to kitsch; how some of us worship idols made of plastic but have been spray-painted in silver. I wanted Andy to be something precious but kitsch, something that doesn't really make sense, something unusual; an installation suggesting everything that is a part of us. Each room or chamber in the Venice Biennale installations provided a different experience related to the world we are living in – the zinc house was like the cage we used to keep our rooster at Seletar Airbase – a combination of reality and fantasy. Through the work, I try to portray Andy as being like "us". Like Andy, we are brought into a very contradictory environment, urban and kampong at the same time.

TBH Some parts of the installation looked like a dream, but also kitschy, like your sculpture of Andy in the gondola.

VL Andy's souvenir (the sculpture) from Venice, the gondolo, you either hate it or you love it; but like the souvenirs we buy as tourists, this work was like a souvenir from Venice to commemorate the participation at the 52ⁿᵈ Venice Biennale of Contemporary Art. Ironically, SAM has purchased for this work collection.

TBH Coming back to today. You thinking of returning to Singapore. How do you see yourself as an artist in the Singapore context now? And, moving forward?

VL I think going away has been an important and valuable experience for me. The only difficult bit was living apart from my family. This opportunity to work outside Singapore was important because it presented an opportunity for me to re-examine my art practice and to further develop my research and work. I wish I had done this earlier; it would have been even more interesting. I still feel that although Sharjah does not have the most interesting art scene in the world, just looking at artists there, looking at their different cultures and motivations, seeing how different their reality is from ours really motivated me. All this pushes me to look at my work from a different perspective.

TBH What are your ideas about contemporary art after so many years, and why do you think contemporary art is still important in a place like Singapore? What is the role of an artist, other than to paint beautiful landscapes of the Singapore River, for example.

Fish Clouds, 2010, oil on canvas, 70 x 100 cm, artist collection

VL In the past 25 years or so as an artist, I would like to think that each piece of work that I have made is contemporary. I believe that my works are closely related to the period and place that I am in. I would like to think that as long as an artist is alive, he is "contemporary" and the work is relevant to a place and its community.

TBH In terms of public and consumer art, there is a genuine shift. People are genuinely interested in The Artists Village and 5ᵗʰ Passage. There is a sense that a lot has been achieved, and yet this achievement is lost, forgotten.

VL Yes, I do feel that there is a change, and acceptance in contemporary art. Definitely a lot has been achieved in terms of its development but little of this has been recognised. Maybe the situation will improve.

The Fine Heart Practice of Vincent Leow

Gilles Massot
Artist

I'm not entirely sure when I met Vincent for the first time. It might well have been on the occasion of a trip to the then St Patrick's Art Centre (later LASALLE College of the Arts) sometime in 1985. Chong Fah Cheong was the lecturer of sculpture then and I vaguely remember meeting him and a few of his students, including Vincent, in an outdoor workshop space at the back of the school.

What I do remember clearly, however, is how and when my friendship and artistic collaboration with Vincent truly kicked off.

It was two years later, and by then St Patrick's had moved to its Telok Kurau campus. A few months before, a realisation had dawned on me: that 1987 was the last year of the millennium with four different digits. Furthermore, each year after that would have at least two similar digits all the way until 2013.

Little did I know that I had somehow stumbled on the time frame now known as the end of the Mayan Calendar. Back then what it meant to me was that the countdown for the still-distant new millennium had begun – and we needed to do something about it. As the world was about to enter a whole new era, the conservation of ancient Asian cultural traditions in the context of an ever-increasingly technological society was an interesting way to kickstart the celebration. Thus, the idea of the 1987 Yin Yang Festival took shape, a festival in which people of different creative fields would exchange their understanding of the age-old philosophy in relation to their contemporary practices.

The idea was met with much enthusiasm and I got, among other things, the National University of Singapore (NUS) Guild House to become the venue and main sponsor of the festival. With all sorts of artists committing to participate, the programme was nicely shaping up. But a pressing question arose: who was going to handle the backstage work? This was when the artist Simon Wong, who had worked on nurturing the idea with me since day one, came up with a bright idea: ask art students from LASALLE and Nanyang Academy of Fine Arts (NAFA) to become that most essential team of people: those working in the background to make things happen.

I had just seen Wim Wenders' film *Wings of Desire* and the day I went to meet the first group of students to present the project, I had asked them to become "the Angels" of the festival. I remember Vincent sitting in the classroom, looking at me, clearly grasping the meaning of the idea. By the end of the meeting, and without me even asking him, he had become the natural leader of the team. And this is what I find most remarkable in Vincent's approach in handling group projects: an unassuming way of taking responsibilities in hand as if he was somehow just having fun.

And indeed the Angels had a lot of fun working on the programme. I knew that things were really on the right track when on the first day of setting up in the Guild House, I saw a beaming Vincent with an electric saw in hand, cutting

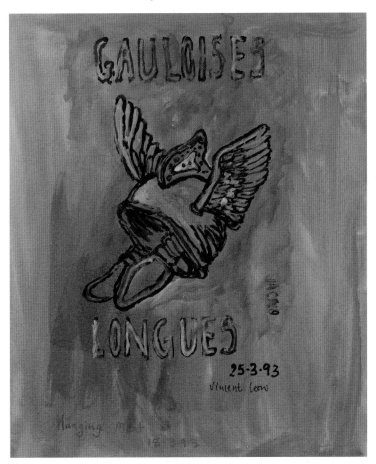

One of the works done by Vincent on a trip to France with Gilles that was later exhibited in Singapore on their return in an exhibition that Gilles curated.
Gauloises Longues, 1993, gouache and ink on paper, 31 x 25 cm, artist collection

out large plywood figures which he and the team had conceived of as a way of animating the club grounds. How on earth had resourceful Vincent managed to gather these sheets of plywood, electric saw and paint, I had no idea, but the result looked really good and the scale of the figures made the most of the open-air environment.

I turned the Angels of the 1987 Yin Yang Festival into the Art Commandos of the 1988 Festival Fringe. The 1988 Singapore Arts Festival Fringe programme is, in my opinion, a turning point in the history of the Singapore arts scene. It has yet to be perceived in the right perspective and not enough has been written about it.

Jessica Leo started the Fringe programme in 1984. After another successful round in 1986, she was given a free hand at putting together an ambitious programme of more than 300 performances over a month, performed by mostly local artistes in all sorts of unconventional venues located island-wide in 1988. That year, the Fringe truly brought the arts to the most remote parts of the nation in a concerted and effective manner. The Fringe also produced the Festival's official opening "City Celebrations" in Marina Square that featured over 3,000 local artistes.

The event was choreographed by the American celebration artiste Marilyn Wood in collaboration with world-renowned French fireworks specialist Pierre-Alain Hubert, with a music score specially composed for the occasion by musician, Joe Peters. Among the lasting influences of the 1988 Fringe, I believe that the artistic emotion – experienced by the crowd of 80,000 gathered on the site of today's Esplanade–Theatres on the Bay – at a time when the art complex was barely at its planning stage, helped to ground the project and make it the success it is today.

Little-known too is the development of the show "Fragile Forest" that was staged at night at various locations next to the animals in the Singapore Zoo, which inspired and eventually became the world-famous Night Safari.

Lastly, the most significant influence of the 1988 Fringe is probably its initiative in spearheading the artistic use of the complex of buildings that had just been vacated by St Joseph's Institution on Bras Basah Road. The deserted school was still filled with objects and furniture that had been left behind. Jessica managed to secure the use of the buildings for the duration of the festival and called for artistic proposals. Artist Tang Mun Kit came up with a proposal for an installation using the discarded objects to create a surrealist evocation of Singapore's leading educational institution. I opted for the school hall and the courtyards as the place to house the Art Commandos.

After the success of the Yin Yang Angels, I conceived the Art Commandos as an artistic action force that would bring art to the streets in the most spontaneous and radical manner: they would choose a target, strike without warning and then leave.

As the overall technical director of the Fringe in 1988, I had little time to get involved in art practice. But sure enough, Vincent took the organisation of this month-long project in hand with ease, efficiently leading the team of students while still allowing them complete artistic expression.

The project started with a week-long art camp in Sentosa that gathered over 30 students from LASALLE, NAFA and Baharuddin Vocational Institute (now known as Temasek Polytechnic). The camp was composed of visual art workshops led by Vincent (and I believe that this might well have been his first experience in "arts education"!) as well as performing arts workshops led by other practitioners such as Christina Sergeant, Barry Cha Cha and Gordon Jansen, the drummer from the blues band Heritage.

I joined them for the first public presentation of their street performance that took place at the Sentosa ferry terminal and was rather impressed with the final result – a sort of modern tribal dance performed to the sound of self-made instruments around a structure made up of bamboo and painted plastic sheets that could be easily moved around.

From there the commandos moved to their "headquarters" in what is today SAM's glass hall. The following weekend saw them perform at the heart of the city along Orchard Road. The second weekend was spent travelling by MRT to destinations such as Toa Payoh Central and Raffles Place, and it concluded with a finale at the Newton Circus Food Centre. The closing weekend saw a final party in the SJI courtyard, with a *topeng* performance by actor Lut Ali. The fact that today Vincent mentions the Art Commandos as his first experience in the performance section of his Curriculum Vitae, and that other members of the team were Josef Ng, Ahmad Abu Bakar and Khairul Anwar Salleh, might give a little idea of the playful and experimental energy the group brought to the Singapore streets then.

I guess that many years and projects later, it is this same light-hearted yet highly efficient approach to management that made Plastique Kinetic Worms (PKW) run so successfully for 10 years. In all my years as a member of PKW and the few other projects I organised with Vincent, such as the New Journey to the West in 1993, what always amazed me was his ability to find solutions instead of just raising problems, combined with the capability of leading a team without ever becoming a "little chief"; if anything, the signs of a true fine heart practitioner.

Knowing Vincent and His Paintings

Ian Woo

Artist

On the subject of myth-making, I sometimes wonder how much of the stories we, as artists, make up overlaps with the everyday personalities of our being. In Paul Auster's novel *Man in the Dark*, we have a situation where August Brill, a bedridden insomniac (recovering from an accident) spends his time imagining a series of dream sequences of a fictional personality involved in an assassination. At some point in this story, reality and fiction overlap, as the imagined persona looks at a website containing Brill's actual curriculum vitae, resulting in a connection. I like to think that if there was a "wall" between reality and fiction, it is probably one that is double-sided, with both sides revealing the same truth. At some point, access to this truth is granted and a relationship between reality and fiction is made, resulting in an extension of the story.

Vincent Leow was a "myth" in my perception from 1990 till 1995; what I knew of him was from the tabloids' coverage of The Artists Village (TAV) as well as from having the opportunity of seeing his paintings (especially *Poultry Shop*, 1989) at The Substation. I had only met him briefly at a party at the TAV-run Hong Bee Warehouse space through Amanda Heng. Both Amanda and Vincent had worn black lipstick and black nail polish, both grinning from ear to ear. On that day, the conversations between Vincent and I were brief and more of a superficial introduction (of course it was, we had to get on with the party!). On another occasion, I remember watching him prepare and make the money suit behind the cell cage and later performing with the items. I did not have an impression of the concept, but I recall I was taken by the shimmering gold of the suit, and I remember how it made Vincent look surreal.

In 1996, I finally got to speak to Vincent again when we were involved in the North East Line MRT public art project. He was the first artist who spoke to me during the early meetings at No. 1 Hampshire Road. I later curated an exhibition, and went to his studio at Telok Kurau to collect his painting *Black Crows*. It was then, on meeting and talking with him, that Vincent ceased to be a "myth".

Yellow Field sketch, 1990, ink and coffee on paper, 22 x 27.8 cm, artist collection

As time went on, I got to know about his gallery Plastique Kinetic Worms (PKW) which he started with 10 other artists and his wife Yvonne, his family and more about his art. We got to know each other well, and we often talked about ideas and "theories", anecdotes in relation to the absurd and strange tales and occurrences in our lives. I remember he shared with me a vision on the appearance of Buddha's head in a woman's home in Thailand, and also his method of cooking spaghetti aglio olio and mentally counting the seconds while frying a steak (5 seconds each side). Both of us share a love for German Expressionist paintings (the whole lot, especially by A.R. Penck and Anselm Kiefer) as well as the Folk Art at Haw Par Villa, and he introduced me to regional artists like Vasan Sitthiket, whom back then, I knew little of.

Vincent is a painter of icons from the contemporary world, from the early paintings of single objects, humans and animals, to the later paintings in which he layered sex and other multiplied situations and motives. The paintings act as some kind of conversation or gossip between its subject matter and its audience. On further examination, the compositions are either depictions of solitary characters and objects in performance that glare at you in their folly or as with the later paintings, are elusive, with the subject matter appearing between patterns, playing a game of hide-and-seek.

There were also some exceptionally romantic paintings done during his studies at the Maryland Institute College of Art in Baltimore. I remember seeing the large epic *Yellow Field* at his Sembawang home. There was something about the ochre yellow created for these works that reminded me of the colour of his money suit. But it was a very well-executed painting, every detail correlated to each other; nothing was there without reason; it had this quality persisting as it was found, there being no affectation of the maker. Vincent understands painting, he knows about the build-up, the slowness of how colours and greys unite to give volume. Most of all, Vincent's application of paint on the surface of the canvas seduces the viewer into realising how aspects of cognitive sight intertwine to give pleasure.

Vincent likes to paint people and animal faces. I once asked him while looking at a series of drawings of a repeated portrait, who he was painting, if it was from some reference. But he said it was all imaginary. Which is probably why the faces of his characters always look peculiar – like its sum of parts is not logical, a juxtaposition – making them almost dumb, like they just had or are having sex and then suddenly lose all sense of edge, like some death and sexual euphoria. This probably adds to the drama within the hierarchy of personalities, so in a sense Vincent is like the Joker in a pack of cards.

Vincent is also an image-maker of the senses; he is instinctive about developing the form of a particular moment. Each time he paints a face, flower or body, the form changes within the context of a given narrative condition; it is a condition of what he wants to see at that given time. In other words, this process gives birth to a myth within the picture.

In relating back to the earlier notion of the "wall" of reality and fiction, I like to think that the artist can choose to see and fulfil within the fictional side of the divide another kind of situation, one that perhaps realises a missing component in reality. Looking from one of Vincent's work to the next, I feel that I have fallen from one dream or nightmare space into another. In all my personal memory of Vincent, the artist becomes part of the extended motivation of his work. Looking through his body of paintings, from the early ones with mostly a single point of view, to the later multiple superimpositions of spaces, there is something like an infinite transition from one dream sequence to the next. As a viewer of his art, I like to think I am participating in making a connection with Vincent's double-sided divide. But I am not sure which is real. For me, it is exactly at this point that Vincent has once again become a myth.

Elephant Dumbo, Dog Andy and Other Fables (Or, About Indirect Discourse)

Milenko Prvacki
Artist and educator

Fables usually encapsulate social issues and critiques. Their messages carry the philosophy of life experiences, attempting to convey moral values, yet mindful that in human life and in nature, the strongest and the smartest are always winners.

My knowledge of Vincent Leow's creative opus started with his 1991 *Dumbo* painting and continued through the most recent sculptures and the variations on the *Andy* themes.

In between these works, we recognise other pillars of his intriguing messages through his swans, macaws, his pet dogs Pablo and Andy, pet rabbits Aladdin and Genie, as well as the other representatives of the animal kingdom which Vincent skillfully uses as instruments of communication with the public, especially with the political milieu.

With his artist direction that employs "conventional" media (colours and materials) through direct discourse to address the public, performance-act being an example, Vincent displays an equal passion and force to communicate. Regardless of the methodology employed, these come across mostly as "imaginative" stories, as humoresque fantasy tools and as intermediary vehicles to translate his reflections.

It is at the most critical moments of his creativity that Vincent once again finds refuge in "indirect discourse". He fully takes advantage of and manipulates animal characters, attributing them human traits, and in doing so making his statement and generating intriguing questions. And as always, the result is in the form of an even more fascinating answer.

Vincent is an artist who publicly (and directly) drank and stored his urine – yet, sometimes chooses (indirectly) to communicate via intermediaries.

His body of work is an intelligent extension of a discourse revolving around a real story without being accused of "polluting" the "calm and decent social structures".

Unlike Hegel, who regarded history as a process of linear development, Nietzsche considered history as a process of spiral development: time moves on, yet everything returns to the same forms. In his book *Thus Spoke Zarathustra*, Nietzsche espoused his thesis that "old" historical chapters are not necessarily better than new ones. Even in his selection of the book title one can see Nietzsche's openness for different non-Western cultures, which are seldom mentioned and referred to by earlier philosophers.

Dumbo, 1991, oil on canvas, 210 x 240 cm, Singapore Art Museum collection

If we consider *perpetuum mobile* (of an artist's work and ideas that are in perpetual motion), the big dilemma regarding paintings, sculptures and prints is that "death" hangs upon us like "the Sword of Damocles" (of the ever-present danger faced by artists and producers of art and culture). And are we talking about the death of the mediums, or about the death of ideas and creation?

Or, is it all only about new stimulation for new birth, of new painting, new sculpture, new prints and new performances?

Vincent, with his ardent passion and a certain whimsical easiness, ignores all those warnings and handles every available media equally, as long as they help him to express his daubs and his worries. His fables are built and recounted in bronze, metal cast, oil paint on canvas or with acrylic on linen.

Isn't each of these paintings just an image done in a different way? Is the narration different if it is told by a different material or a different modality?

The brush – once upon a time – was itself a big technological discovery, just as today's video camera. The camera as a tool is still developing and there is no end to its improvement. That never ends. We will always want newer, better cameras.

Vincent is continuously positioned on the side of the creative restless; his attempt to approach history, geography and social issues is about working and chipping away at them constantly, and it shows that he deeply enjoys his work.

By painting, printing, putting up an installation or being a performance artist, Vincent has always given way to provocation – to himself and all of us.

He is, in fact, a dreaming artist and a fairytale artist, as "Andy" is the "spokesperson" for human qualities and defaults, as Moby Dick is the epitome of wisdom, memory and remembrance.

Vincent's early "fight" and today's compilations are actually his struggle against stupidity and is a form of empowerment, a laugh against death. Quite enough elements remind us of cyclic history (a theory which dictates that the major forces that motivate human actions return in a cycle) and of its emerging and rapidly developing rhythm.

We should be aware as well of hybridism in his artwork, reflected in the various media from which he freely creates his imagery. There is Pop-Art, primitive art, repetitive motifs, the easiness of German Expressionism and the smooth, sophisticated new technological edge of "made objects".

Vincent's quiet and Zen-like wisdom is getting deeper with age and experience, yet at the same time, he interacts with the public through his works.

In all his past works, I get caught and get pulled into Vincent's magical world. The energy driving him in his young days of artistry in engaging the public and becoming involved in his performances has now been replaced by the wisdom of a storyteller.

I remember once in a show at The Substation Gallery, he requested that Brother Joseph McNally communicate with him only through the mobile phone, despite the fact they were in the same room. That was a "sub-cultural" revolt of Vincent's, a rebelliousness against new habits and urban behaviours, and a form of indirect communication. For Vincent, the media is the new way to interact with the public, and in a society not accustomed to provocation and imagery, he created an awareness of the exchange of reality when two people correspond.

It is very rare that the enthusiasm at the start of an artistic career lasts. Usually it happens that this enthusiasm is replaced by intelligent and contemplated actions, a completely different manifestation in temperament.

Vincent is open to all methods of engaging audiences as long as they question the right issues and they communicate clear messages. Vincent, however, has never changed in his persistent, ever-challenging methods, positioning himself as an observer in society.

The materials he used have changed and interchanged... (pencil, bronze, colour, ink, stone, toys...). Yet, Vincent, as an artist, has remained the same, continuously creating assemblages of utopic ingredients.

Unfortunately, nowadays, no one can grow up with tales and stories. They are replaced by cheap and lazy-thinking substitutes.

Vincent Leow: Coffee Talk (1992)

Ray Langenbach
Artist, researcher

During the final night of 1992, Vincent Leow served up his *Coffee Talk* performance. The performance was part of Body Fields, the New Year's Eve festival of art and performance presented at 5th Passage – located in the fifth-floor passageway in Parkway Parade shopping centre, between the shops and the car park.

Six years later, Vincent wrote a description of the performance:

"I used my body and an installation set like a café – the café as a metaphor of my studio... I began the performance by greeting the 20–30 people in the audience. I then sat down and started addressing them on issues of art and other irrelevant stuff. At that time it wasn't important that they understand me. I wanted them to hear sound and noises coming from my vocal chords... I wanted the audience to experience a piece of nonsense. After all, is there such a thing as significant nonsense?

After my address, I got up from my chair, picked up a coffee cup and pissed into the cup on the stage. With the cup full of urine, I made a toast to the audience and drank it. After consuming the urine, I sat down and started cutting locks of my hair and placed them in several envelopes addressing it to several people in the art scene, distributing them to the audience, ending the performance.

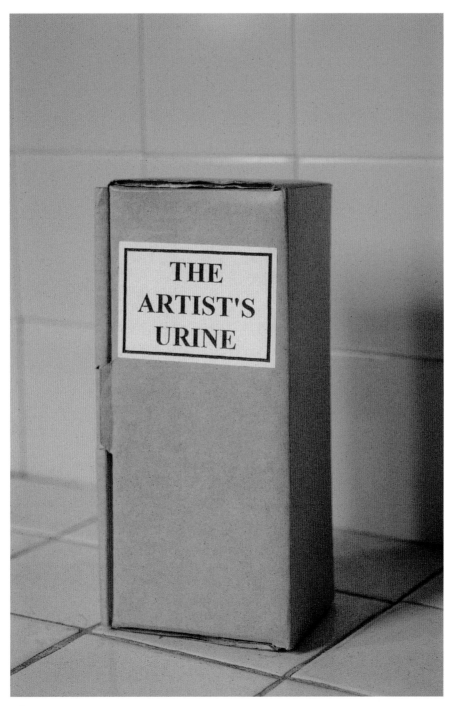

A "limited edition" of *The Artist's Urine*

The performance was a raw, random event and appeared meaningless. I was concerned with the issue of self-consumption, using the urine as a metaphor for the artist as both producer and the consumer. At the end of the performance the audience applauded..."

(The above was from an email correspondence with the artist, 11/12/98.)

Falling into the late modernist performance tradition of Body Art, Vincent's performance speaks to the excess of the body and its "ruminations": its behaviours, bodily products (urine, hair) and physical as well as cognitive products (speech, performance structure). Vincent installed a cup, chair and table – all popular signifiers of the kopitiam that was once a public site for conviviality and consumption. By 1991/92, the traditional kopitiam had been transformed into an empty brand name for restaurant chains in the shopping malls (such as Marine Parade) that had displaced the small shops, in much the same way that it appeared as an empty signifier in Vincent's performance.

But the political importance of *Coffee Talk* in contemporary Singapore was not clear for another year. Despite it being a tradition in some Asian countries to drink one's own urine for health, Vincent's simple act became an opportunity for the press to sell newspapers, and *Coffee Talk* set off a chain reaction in Singapore's cultural scene that would be felt for years.

In July 1993, Vincent capped *Coffee Talk* with another performance entitled *IO*, at the National Gallery Theatrette. Vincent began by announcing that the event was a "workshop" in which he wanted to "talk about meaning and non-meaning". He then said, "I am an art salesman... an art prostitute." He passed out blindfolds with "I" printed over one eye and "O" over the other, and led the audience through a series of games distinguishing meaning from non-meaning. This was followed by an ambling, periodically confused and impassioned response to the press coverage on his urine consumption in *Coffee Talk*. A number of members of the audience were critical of his passivity in the face of the sensationalist media accounts of his work, questioning whether Vincent was revelling a bit too much in his notoriety. The press reports had dilated the performance for public consumption, and he became both artist and object of cultural fascination for the general public.

Subsequently, Vincent launched a "limited edition" of his bottled urine. Packaged in a small cardboard box, entitled *The Artist's Urine*, each of the bottles was labelled, signed and numbered by the artist, priced at $30. Identified as a "Product of Singapore", the item clearly established the work's ironic value. *IO* has two modern antecedents: the bottle of urine in Kurt Schwitters'

Merzbau installation, and Piero Manzoni's *Artist's Shit* (1961), which was packaged in ninety 30-gram cans, to be sold at the current price of gold.

In the local context, Vincent's work focuses our attention on the incessant dialectics between scene and obscene in the Singapore public sphere: that which can be staged versus those bodily processes, acts or ideas that are deemed too private or sensitive for public viewing. Vincent's performance, perhaps inadvertently, joined the global feminist discourse in circulation at 5th Passage in 1993–1994 that framed the body as a political site.

Health tonic or not, by drinking his urine in public, Vincent was seen by the press to have transgressed normative behaviour. The spectacle around the Body Fields event and *Coffee Talk* focused on issues that were part and parcel of experimental art and performance art in the 1990s – politics of the body, transgression, obscenity, identity, ideology and the relative autonomy and marginality of the community of artists – and brought these issues not only into public view, but also into the view of the government. This would be made clear precisely one year later at the next (and last) New Year's exhibition, Artists' General Assembly (1993/4) at 5th Passage. The press repeated the sensational coverage of performance art, during which *Coffee Talk* was recalled. This coverage was then used by the government to justify the subsequent decade-long ban on the licensing and funding of performance art and Forum Theatre.

Vincent Leow
and The Bestial Body

Isabel Ching
Art curator and writer

Andy's Addiction (1996), *Bombs Away* (1996) and *Mr Peanut* (1996) all play on the mechanism of duality. Despite the centrality of the main figure and the paring down of competing elements in these paintings, it is impossible to articulate a consistent message or fix an identity in these works. Instead, what is conveyed is the existential angst exemplified by the ambivalent imagery of a harlequin being conjoined to a tamed animal's (or part-animal's) body.

Welding together the separate and distinct social, cultural and political (not to mention biological) genealogies of the different entities is like a treacherous, spiked dog collar. The exaggerated armour is also a mark of domestication. It contributes to a sense of inchoate anxiety in an encounter with monstrosity and marks out the hybrid's weak spot. The animals chosen – a chicken and the family dog – are far from threatening. They are the most ordinary and humble of creatures, caught in a one-way power relationship with the human: the chicken is bred as fodder for the masses while the pet dog is in need of sustenance and affection from man.

Andy's Addiction, 1996, oil on canvas, 120 x150 cm, private collection

In the language of painting, a rather sympathetic and naturalistic rendering of the bestial body is contrasted with the flat and graphic form depicting the human face, further splitting the figure into two incompatible parts. Affinities are more easily felt for the bestial body, which acquires mass, texture and pliability than for the white clown face whose lips are fixed in a rigid, teeth-baring grin. That being the case, the repeated clown face in these works is nevertheless capable of unlimited expressions – ranging from the sinister (*Bombs Away*) to the inscrutable (*Mr Peanut*) and the desperate (*Andy's Addiction*) – with all the dramatic elements retained. The paintings therefore are not founded on pastiche and subversion, but function as portraits that divulge aspects of personality and psychological strangleholds.

Viewed as a suite, the works see the harlequin act out his talent as a chameleon, assuming different guises and manners to get what he wants. Even the fool's cap that marks him out yields to the animals' forms – two prongs as ears for the dog and three prongs in a row for the chicken's comb. Although traditionally only a servant, the harlequin is dexterous, disruptive and rebellious, giving rise to boisterous, comical effects – the consummate entertainer! But here, his agility seems weighed down by the clumsy and contradictory mutations that he gets himself into, his gleefully pathetic disposition propping up an uneasy hilarity.

Self-ridicule is never far away. Not only do the faces in the paintings bear a caricaturised resemblance to the artist, but invoking the harlequin or clown signals that an alter ego may be in operation. The figure of the harlequin or clown is useful for representing the divided self, examining identity and exploring the dichotomy between appearance and reality: behind the smiling, public face could be hiding a maniacal, traumatised character (such as the Joker in the *Batman* comics), or sadness, pain and other complex emotions, or something else altogether. In this case, the artist doesn't resolve the enigma, and pathways for probing further into the personality aspects portrayed are blocked. The harlequin-animal hybrid subject is not only irrevocably split, but mutely so. It hovers over physically and psychologically indeterminate terrain, augmented by how the figure "floats" from the ground, rendering uncertain the relationships between the figure and the bordering-on-decorative ground, the real and the imagined, surface and content.

The magical and shamanistic potentials of the hybrid, as well as mythical gods and monsters, of which the Sphinx, Hanuman, Ganesha and the Harpy are examples, are not so much tapped on as inverted in their impotent, contemporary manifestation. Satire and mockery form the main tenor of these works as the dog-man acts insipidly, a servile lackey to gratify libidinal appetites, while the chicken-man absurdly and arrogantly plays predator and lord of the skies!

On display is a bestiality (or a human culture) that is mediocre, ignoble, masochistic and grasping. This is not a bestiality that needs to be controlled by rational laws and civilisation, but one that arises precisely from the crisis of a bridled and over-engineered reality. It is vulnerable to crude mechanisms of control and brow-beating, and constantly haunted by the spectres of insecurity and tragic impotence. This doesn't make for particularly attractive *dramatis personae* in a play about stunted action, thwarted nature and ludicrous posturing. Garuda and Centaur they are surely not, but as recent inventions in a secular and scientifically advanced age, they are at least appropriate to certain local matrices.

MTV Flash-frozen: The Crystallisation of the Moving Image

Pwee Keng Hock
Gallery owner

The evolution of Vincent the Painter follows a certain distinct lineage, as individualistic as Vincent the Sculptor, or Vincent the Performance Artist. Four Eyes, Cloudy Skies (2001) marked his fourth solo painting exhibition in Singapore, his first three marked by Donkeys, Elephants and the Three-Legged Toad (1992) with Shenn's Fine Arts, Chop Suey (1994) with Art-2 and Falling Bones, Hungry Chillies (1996) at The Substation Gallery respectively.

Vincent began painting with a vengeance during his Masters at the Maryland Institute College of Art, USA (1989–1991), after having trained ostensibly as a sculptor at the LASALLE College of the Arts, Singapore (1985–1987). His paintings merrily distort perspective and anatomy, can be garish in their colour schemes and blithely dismiss a staid academicism. In its naïve expressionism, Vincent's paintings find familiar echoes throughout Southeast Asia, such as the work of Heri Dono and Eddie Hara in Indonesia (whom Vincent met when they all were students), Vasan Sitthiket in Thailand, perhaps less so with Tan Chin Kuan in Malaysia and Charlie Co in the Philippines. Vincent confesses to having been influenced by folk painting through his travels – Thai temple paintings, Balinese *wayang* paintings and Indian folk art. Quick, simple gestures succinctly capture the human figure, with colour deftly filled in: the idea or the essence is more important than the mode of depiction.

Images from popular culture such as Chinese icons and brand labels were prevalent in his earlier paintings, but are brandished sparingly in the 2001 exhibition in which spaceships and dinosaurs make incongruous appearances. Vincent's fondness for animals transmogrified into a series of human-headed creatures in *Falling Bones, Hungry Chillies*, and certainly animals abound in *Four Eyes, Cloudy Skies* but they are less anthropomorphised now, save for a dextrous horse in *Circus Rabbit*.

Curious images abound in all of Vincent's paintings, and the temptation is to read messages and hidden meanings, as befitting his perceived status as an "angry young man" of Singaporean art. The epithet sits uneasily with him: notwithstanding 5th Passage infamy, he will admit to veiled comment and barbed statements in his earlier work, but these have largely been personal responses, relating to arts issues for instance, not scathing social commentary nor political invective. He confesses that he hates making his statements explicit, as if trying too hard to push a message. Nevertheless, Vincent was indeed a significant voice in the new cultural energy that swept through the Singapore art scene in the late 1980s and early 1990s, which saw the birth of Singapore theatre, and in the visual arts, the introduction of installation and performance art. As a key member of The Artists Village (TAV), Head of Sculpture at the LASALLE-SIA College of the Arts (as it was known then), and a founder of artist-run spaces such as the now defunct Utopia and Plastique Kinetic Worms (PKW), his neo-

Falling Bones, Hungry Chillies, 1996, oil on canvas, 120 x 150 cm, private collection

expressionist influences live on in younger artists such as Lam Hoi Lit, Chua Chye Teck and Benjamin Puah.

Whither painting in the new millennium? Vincent bemoans the relative lack of inspiration in Singapore for the dearth of exciting painting, but admits it is the price we pay for prosperity and a stable political climate.

Having spent a residency in Yogyakarta in 2000, Vincent has observed that political turmoil in Indonesia has thrown up strong narrative work and extensive social commentary where figuration seems obligatory. "It's as if the minute you paint social commentary, it sells," he observes, musing that this regional trend has become the new exoticism for collectors, many of whom are still foreign expatriates or Western-educated locals. Socio-political images are now easily used as a selling point, he opines, citing the revolutionary images of Chinese artist Wang Guangyi or the peasant-poverty issues of Filipino Nunelucio Alvarado at the gallery Atelier Frank and Lee.

What, however, can the Singaporean painter use as narrative? Can the *ennui* be relooked, examined, interpreted and dealt with in a uniquely Singaporean way? Vincent realises that it is incumbent upon the Singaporean artist now to create his own opportunities, rather than to let the situation dictate. Abstraction is one solution: the 2000 Singapore leg of the Philip Morris ASEAN Regional Art Awards in which Vincent was a judge turned up a proportionately greater amount of abstract works, in contrast to other works from the region, where figuration was prevalent.

In his paintings of 2000–2001, Vincent has been consciously seeking to create paintings which create the visual "experience" for the viewer. Independent of medium, style or content, a successful painting speaks to its audience and evokes a visual sensation which speaks of the artist, his feelings and of the painting itself. Until he was able to view an actual painting of Jackson Pollock for instance, Vincent could not honestly understand the attractions of drip painting and abstract expressionism. Unlike several artists who manage to latch onto a successful individualistic trait for recognition or commercialism, Vincent has always eschewed painting according to theme, series or formula. What he now knows he wants is to provide the "experience", he admits, not that he necessarily knows how. With this realisation, it becomes difficult to paint, as he never knows what the eventual outcome may be, although there is painful deliberation in the painting process. A painting for Vincent is finished only when he senses completion between himself and the painting, and he only hopes that he can create a similar relationship between the viewer and the exhibited product.

The Four Eyes, Cloudy Skies exhibition functions as a sort of stock-taking for the painter through the last year or so. The paintings are replete with objects and discrete images, for Vincent cannot avoid figuration as a means of expressing himself on canvas. There is, however, a much heavier density of disparate images which are essentially unrelated to each other, and this in itself may function as a form of abstraction, rather than non-objective expression which Vincent has no affinity for. Using film as an analogy, he asks: is it possible to develop characters without actually telling a story between figures, to avoid using the painting as a freeze-frame of a narrative? Vincent intends for each image to lead the viewer from one personal voyage of discovery of the painter's intentions (or lack of them) to another. For his current work, inevitable links are created in one's mind in an attempt to comprehend each juxtaposed image, and this forces the relationship with the painting to be more involved, more participatory for the viewer. The emphasis is on the paintings, the process of painting, the layering of images, the spatial relationships of objects and the connectivity of images, whether real or imagined. Optical effects such as the interweaving of hoops and lines, or the dinosaur and lines in *Lucky Number*, or the concentric circles in *Digestive* are given prominence, and the viewer has to develop his own points of reference in ordering his perception of the images – foreground: background; focal point: counterpoint; subject: *leitmotif.*

A number of commonalities abound: repeated images and motifs are used to pattern the canvases, alternately superposed or as background to the more individual images. The woodcut of a bespectacled man (no, it is *not* meant as a self-portrait!) glances somewhat disapprovingly from *Flying Barman* and returns in other canvases; clouds, dots and hoops alternately disrupt image connectivity, yet hold individual paintings together. In *Dirty Dreams*, a central whitening gives an unexpected prophylactic appearance to the hoops, irreverent, yet appropriate! The rural setting of the artist's home in Seletar camp provides much source material for several paintings – insects, animals and plants are found in *Cowboy*, *Digestive* and *Circus Rabbit*, as if to fictionalise the ordinary organism and raise the images to mythological status (a familiar theme of Falling Bones, Hungry Chillies). Oblique references to the environment are observed in the image of Senoko Power Station in *Circus Rabbit* and pipes discharging effluent in *Dirty Dreams*. In a separate series of smaller canvases, quotations culled from the newspaper and media are overlaid upon the paintings, inviting again queries of connectivity between words and pictures. It behooves us to remind ourselves, however, that while Vincent has a criterion for the images he chooses, he has, like MTV, selected them for visual impact rather than as a reference to the song he sings.

In Southeast Asia, history has always been told through drawings and pictures. For a modern day scribe such as Vincent, the personal history told in Four Eyes, Cloudy Skies is reflective of the struggle for a Singaporean voice in painting, amidst the powerful, unbridled expression in our region. Singaporeans flit from event to event, image to image, moment to moment in a runaround struggle that we call our life. Looking back a millennium later, what history of Singapore will Vincent's paintings have foretold?

First published in 2001 for Four Eyes, Cloudy Skies exhibition, Atelier Frank & Lee.

Vincent Leow: Mock Ducks and Manicured Poodles

Ho Tzu Nyen
Artist and film-maker

There is something distinctly disturbing about the figures that populate the paintings of Vincent Leow's "Mock Ducks & Manicured Poodles" exhibition at Jendela Visual Art Space @ Esplanade. In *Last Wish* (2004), the ultimate moment of a man holding a dying comrade is sketched in black and the outlines resemble the flat "iconicity" of Chinese Revolution woodcuts. Any possibility of emotional resonance with these cutout figures is disrupted by the huge lurid flowers erupting from the surface like so many sores, just as any potential narrative coherence between the theme of death and flowers is dispelled by a third image floating between the two – a head sketched in blue, seemingly caught in the moment of wavering between looking and turning away. This blue man could well be the spectator who found himself oscillating between attraction and repulsion, and attention and distraction, before these 13 paintings.

In *Dinner Date* (2004), a lady wearing a *cheongsam* and a man in a suit preside over a typical "bourgeois" dinner table, complete with wine and cigarettes in hand, as a Greek column hovers in the backdrop – a deluge of multicultural signs swept together by the flow of capital. Again, huge flowers in the background struggle to resonate with this depicted scene – either as enlargements of the floral motifs on the lady's *cheongsam* or as suggestions of an erotic undercurrent. Yet, in the age of MTV, where images come together without the necessity of coherence, we are inclined to see that the various motifs in these paintings fall apart; that the narrative cannot hold. An irreducible distance persists between the two planes, just as an infinite distance seems to exist between the couple, regardless of how closely they are seated together.

Pastiche or the coming together of disparate things that do not necessarily enter into a meaningful relationship has, for some time, been the *modus operandi* of Vincent's painterly practice. In this exhibition, pastiche operates vertically – with the superimposition of clearly delineated motifs. But pastiche, too, must be understood to be operative at another level: in the resonance of these paintings with those of Sigmar Polke and David Salle. It is as though Vincent's uncompromising struggle to localise these influences, to make them his own, translates into the fascinating difficulty involved in looking at them – a difficulty which makes them extremely compelling.

Courtesy of Art Asia Pacific
Art Asia Pacific, Winter 2005, Issue No. 43, page 77.

Dinner Date, 2004, oil on canvas, 150 x 180 cm, artist collection

No Requiem for Andy
(d.o.b. unknown–2009)

Lindy Poh
Art consultant

Brief notes on the various phases of Vincent Leow's practice through a survey of the appearance of Andy Man-Dog in his works.

Companion, guardian, muse and magician – Andy Warholy (or Andy Man-Dog) – artist Vincent Leow's black mongrel dog has ruled the artist's keynote pieces for over a decade. Depictions of Andy have surfaced in a number of works, from Vincent's *Flying Circus* series of the 1990s to the five-room installation in the Singapore Pavilion at the Venice Biennale 2007, to an extensive showing in *Andy's Pranks and Swimming Lessons* in Beijing in 2007, as well as exhibitions in Seoul 2007 and London 2008/9.

Andy Warholy (obviously inspired by Warhol's name [1928–1987]) was so named in tribute to the artist-icon who had influenced Vincent – not just in evolving Vincent's Pop-Art sensibilities but in shaping Vincent's "ideology" of contemporary art and its intersections in business and commerce – ideologies made legendary by Warhol. This was apparent following Vincent's 1992 performance in which he drank his urine and extended the gesture through the packaging and sale of bottles of his urine. The spontaneous performance earned him public notoriety and not a little trouble with the authorities. It was the subsequent "branding and trademarking" of the spontaneous performance using packaged urine that epitomised Vincent's artful handling of his underground, subversive practices, and his Warholian grasp of the mechanics of market consumption and its desire for scandal and controversy that offered the audience-consumer his "products" without irony.

Andy was absent from Vincent's early canvases – the dog joined the Leow household only in the 1990s – by which time Vincent had already incorporated animals like his pet rooster in his works during The Artist Village (TAV) days. Vincent's early paintings were raw and visceral, bearing the influence of German painters such as Georg Baselitz and A.R. Penck as well as the Russian Chaim Soutine. These gestural paintings saw the emergence of a style of paintings in

Holy Lounge (installation, detail), 2007, photograph, 90 x 120 cm,
Singapore Art Museum collection, donation by Chua Soo Bin

Singapore that spoke of unapologetic aggression, blatant sexuality and emotional temperament.

Vincent's later paintings assumed several shifts, particularly during and after his art studies in the USA where he graduated in 1991. The works of this period were broadly marked "urban street style" with inflections of Neo-Surrealism; others were touched by a Pop-Art sensibility, a taste for kitsch and a highly individual visual vocabulary that involved the mixing of imagery and tropes. These manifested in performances, installations, sculptures, digital and mixed-media works – prompting art writers to describe his practice as exemplifying "post-modern" visual strategies.

Vincent explored single-animal subjects in several paintings from the 1990s – penguin, giraffe and elephant for instance, and then later "cross-bred" them to fabricate fantastic creatures, such as those in *The Flying Circus* series of the mid 1990s. It was in this series that Andy Man-Dog debuts. At that time, Vincent co-ran the alternative (and now defunct) artist's space Utopia with ceramicist-performance artist Jason Lim. Both Vincent and Jason as well as their respective partners were housemates, and it was Jason who first brought Andy home (although the Leows subsequently adopted the mongrel). Curators and art writers have speculated that Andy Man-Dog is Vincent's self-portrait, alter-ego or second self. The artist himself has remained deliberately ambivalent about the issue in several interviews, enabling Andy Man-Dog to take on a life of its own over the years.

Andy Man-Dog is frequently depicted as maniacally grinning (not unlike the wicked face-splitting grin of James O'Barr's *The Crow* character or Tsugumi Ohba's Ryuk in *Death Note*). It is not a surprising device used by Vincent and highly effective in suggesting the continuity of certain narratives and motifs, not unlike the strategies used in serial advertisements or pulp fiction to stimulate curiosity and hopefully, addiction. Vincent has been held up as a remarkable imagist and an absorbing storyteller who dips into an astonishing range of images from popular culture: cinema, MTV as well as political propaganda.

The deployment of Andy as a "repeat" character or protagonist in seemingly endless plots lends coherence, sets rhythm and creates a sense of familiarity for the viewer. This is nowhere more critical than in Vincent's installation for the Singapore Pavilion at the Venice Biennale in 2007. Spanning five chambers at the neo-Gothic palazzo – the venue for the Singapore Pavilion at the biennale – the entirety of Vincent's ambitious project was titled *Andy's Wonderland*. Vincent was one of four Singapore artists (the other three being Tang Da Wu, Jason Lim and Zulkifle Mahmod) whose offerings at the pavilion mobilised a diverse range of influences, from Venetian mythology to pulp fiction, cinema, retro-futurism and kitsch aesthetics to Asian literature and philosophies.

The curatorial concept of the Singapore pavilion was rooted in *lo real maravilloso* ("a marvellous reality") – the idea of the marvellous, the fabulous or phantasmagorical, deeply embedded in a version of reality. In the spirit of the fabulous beasts of Venetian fables, *Andy's Wonderland* featured Andy and Hawk (the Man-Bird) engaging in activities of *delire lucide* (lucid delirium), prompted by the idea of "the-marvellous-in-the-everyday".

Vincent's *mise-en-scène* for each room conveyed a sense of containment and regulation – with Hawk and Andy paradoxically reigning supreme with their inimitable grins. The installation included a sub-urban zinc hut (*Hawk Suburbia Lawn*) for Hawk, a padded asylum (*Andy Padded Cell*) and a glass hot-house for incubating Andy (*Harry Pet Hotel*), a cemetery with scattered human hair (*Haven Rapture Garden*) and finally, a portrait gallery (*Holy Lounge*).

The last chamber, *Holy Lounge*, featured an elegant photographic portrait of Andy Warholy on a gentleman's armchair, shot in collaboration with Singapore photographer Cher Him. Vincent had originally planned a much more extensive profiling for Andy that included a short film of him flamboyantly arriving in a yacht in Venice and engaging in various ventures on the island. Whilst this did not materialise for the Biennale, it expressed the artist's intentions of layering and building upon the fiction of the "Life and Times of Andy".

Vincent had, following the Venice Biennale, continued to fictionalise the life of Andy – creating the ambitious painting-sculpture installation for *Andy's Pranks and Swimming Lessons* for the premiere in Beijing later the same year. More scenarios for Andy emerged in projects and exhibitions that came hot on the heels of the Biennale. By the time Andy Warholy (the actual mongrel) passed away in 2009, spending his last days with Vincent's dealer and friend Chua Soo Bin (with the Leows' temporary relocation to the Sharjah in the UAE), it had become apparent that Andy Man-Dog had acquired an invincible youth and longevity that only art and effective image-making could secure.

Material, Culture and Everyday Life

Yvonne Lee
Art consultant

Art always has its relevance to life, as can be seen in how people relate to a creation, or how artists sift through their everyday happenings for inspirations. Having said that, I doubt one can be flippant enough to say "Art is Life and Life is Art". I am simply trying to bring forth the issues that have always been left unnoticed – things that we have started to ignore and taken for granted – like that of space and time. That is perhaps what Vincent Leow is attempting to bring across – his experiences in another space and, somehow, another "time". He has experienced the difference between two countries: from an island confronted with urbanisation and globalisation, and later, experiencing life in Yogyakarta, a society that is conscious of the deafening effects of globalisation, but maintains its traditions and culture. Throughout his two-month residency in Yogyakarta in 2000, awarded by the Cemeti Foundation, Vincent observed and absorbed his surroundings, his new environment.

Big Head, Little People, 1999, cast aluminium and wood, Singapore Art Museum collection

To an extent, Vincent has been both amazed and impressed by the fact that even though Javanese society in Yogyakarta is flourishing, the trail of charm and mysticism is left to be explored and understood. He was housed in a modern home in Yogyakarta, but witnessed the various traditions still being practiced there. Vincent develops the content of his works from his responses to and experiences of the everyday social realities. His approach and treatment are, most of the time, marked by a sense of humour. He sometimes delves into the realms of the imaginary in his selection of materials. He also strongly believes in communication. He is constantly in search of interaction and the opportunity to further expand and exchange thoughts with the public as well as with other artists.

His past works have seen him explore images and popular icons such as the cloned animal, Dolly the Sheep, and using her as a metaphor of social concern. *Mountian Cow Milk Factory* (deliberate misspelling) in 1998 was one such work. He created a series of identical cows (both in a series of paintings and sculptures) which travelled to various venues before ending up in a sculpture park in Siena, Italy. In *Mountian Cow Milk Factory*, Vincent was preoccupied with the idea of mass production and the globalisation of culture. His intention behind exhibiting the series in several places was to provoke his audience to engage in the issue of location.

Since then, Vincent has started working on images by the multiples. His later series titled *Big Head, Little People* (1999) was derived from a Chinese expression: "Someone with a big ego with ill intention". It was an installation consisting of identical little men made out of clay and a larger-than-life wood sculpture of a human head on a table measuring 3 ft by 3 ft. The entire table was filled to the edges with little men, with the head sitting prominently in the centre. The installation sees the representation of power and ego that exist in our society. It explores the ills of the society that we live in, questioning the realities and conflicts. And how, despite the awareness of our flaws, one does nothing about the state of our society and simply ignores it.

The idea of *Caged Feet* (2000), re-installed in the *Feet Remembered* (2010) installation, is a continuation of what Vincent has been exploring but in another context, from another perspective. Though he is very much focused on the issue of tradition and culture, and the ever-changing environment in our society, his primary concern is still the social consciousness of art that forms the expression of social existence in every place. He believes that in the metaphorical sense, art cannot be a question of intent. It is how one experiences the sublime, or does not, according to one's fate and character.

On The Artworks by Vincent Leow

Isak Berbic

Artist, writer and educator

There is a line from Kafka's novel *The Trial* in which the protagonist is indicted by an obscure authority for a crime never revealed to him or to the reader. I quote here from memory: "One might say that this is not a trial at all. It is only a trial if I recognise it as such." This is the unique state of contemporary art today: once we are in the process of reading an artwork, we submit to partake in the trial of contextual rhetoric that generates the work into existence. In postmodernity, the abyss of contexts, artistic methods, meanings and particularities have fractured the validating cannon. Vincent Leow's overarching artistic project of the last two decades is situated within this contemporary discourse of postmodernity. His complex use of art historical tropes, pop culture and personal narratives positions his practice in contest to official narratives and political, social and aesthetic ideologies. On the state of postmodernism, Hal Foster asked 27 years ago: how can we transgress the transgressive? Vincent's work poignantly addresses these very relevant issues in contemporary

Black Face, 2010, oil on canvas, 60 x 45 cm, artist collection

art today. His practice has developed a continuity in language but at the same time it does not trust its own devices, its etymology or assertions. One project proposes its own mythology, while the next may re-evaluate it. His politics refer to a particularity, yet they do not rely on it to produce meaning. His conceptual approach leads the selection of medium, yet there is evident discipline, formalism, manual dexterity and mastery of craft.

On Painting, in the Recent Paintings by Vincent Leow

Vincent's recent pieces predominantly take place on canvas and paper. He demonstrates a contemplative study of the painting process and the ability of material to assemble meaning. The images are stark, reminiscent of Hitchcock or Film Noir sets. Usually a human figure, an object, a dog or a rabbit is positioned as a central visual element. These icons refer back to his earlier works like the Andy projects, early paintings that included animals, masks and body parts. On these new canvases there is a reduction of detail with a shallow pictorial space and a minimal, base backdrop. The figures pose on their theatrical stage, communicating to the viewer a psychological state through an exaggerated posture.

There is a liquid quality to the paint laid on the canvas, as if it has not yet hardened into solid matter. Dense smears are pushed with the brush like rhythmic swim strokes following imaginary borders that guide the paint. The strokes form structures which do not assemble patterns but piece together a whole shape. These shapes are silhouetted iconic referents to a figure or humanness. Vincent refuses realistic mimesis of the traditionalist portrait; the semblance to the human figure is symbolic. However, paint is a viscous material. It appears fleshy, sweaty, oily and greasy. Its sheen and mucus-like surface is still life, mortal, as if prepared by a taxidermist. The way Vincent paints the hands suggests that they are cut off from the rest of the body. The isolated flesh-toned hands attached to the black figures appear as fragments of skin placed over the skeleton. This symbolic reference points us to interpret the hands as the only part left, that which is human tissue.

The head and torso are made up of liquid black paint resembling petroleum. The shape of the head is a mass of black with the features in the face represented by brush strokes delineating the mouth, the nose and the eyes. One has to peer more closely to inspect the black-on-black information, only discernible as light reflects the texture from the glossy surfaces. The landscape behind the figure is thin. It spreads to demonstrate atmosphere, as if gas has dried on the canvas. Around the silhouette are sneezes of shooting, spraying paint. Their image functions in multiple registers. The first purpose is representative. They suggestively bring to life the inert figures. The figures stand cramped still, but the spraying paint is repelled from their interior, caught in this frozen photographic moment. The paint protrudes outward, like a dog shaking water off his coat. The second purpose is deconstructive. The spray drops reveal their very painterly materiality to us like bolts that hold the machine together. They directly announce that this is a painting. We can deduce that these drops fell from the brush and gravity took them from the motors of the wrist by the law of falling bodies before finally terminating on the canvas surface, where the liquid substance flattened to become crust following its impact.

Yellow Field, 1990, oil and mixed media on canvas, 180 x 250 cm, artist collection

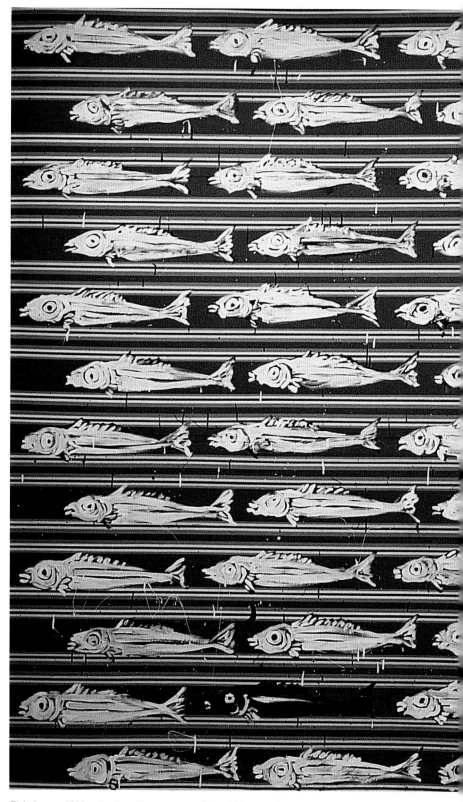

Fishabunga, 1990, mixed media on canvas, 250 x 180 cm, artist collection

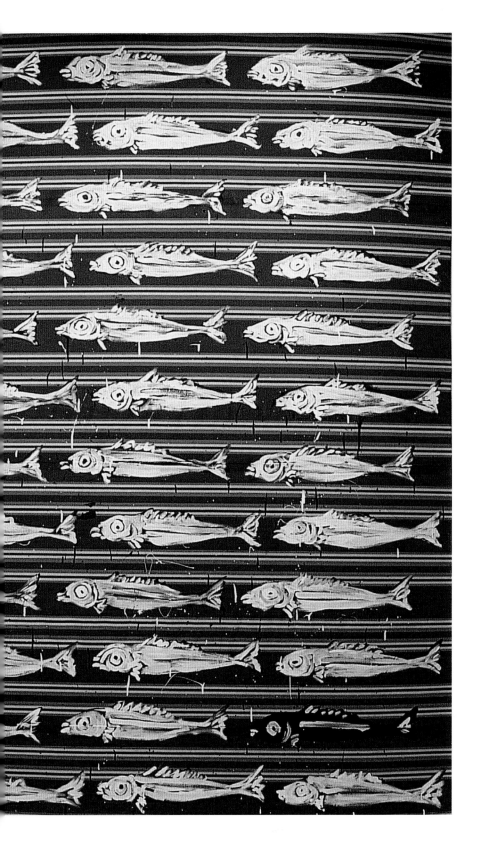

Aladdin & Genie, 1994, oil on canvas, 101 x 121 cm, artist collection

Mr Peanut, 1996, oil on canvas, 86 x 127 cm, artist collection

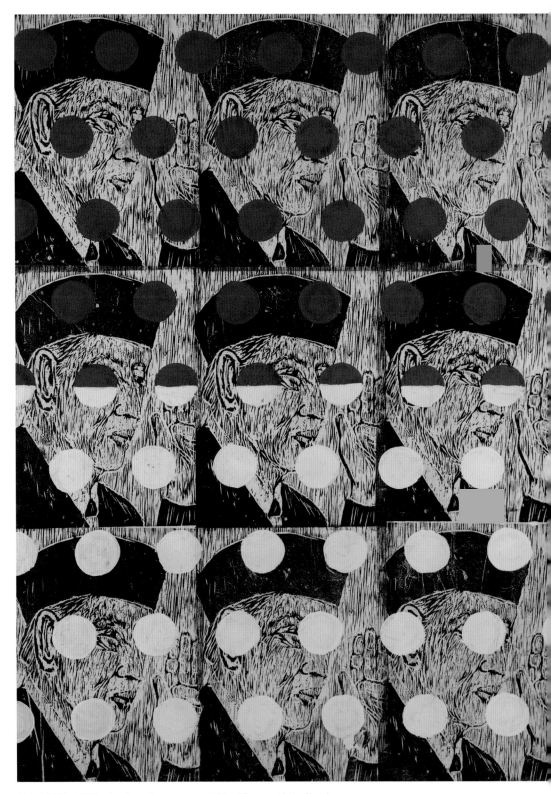

Red & White, 2000, mixed media on canvas, 120 x 90 cm, artist collection

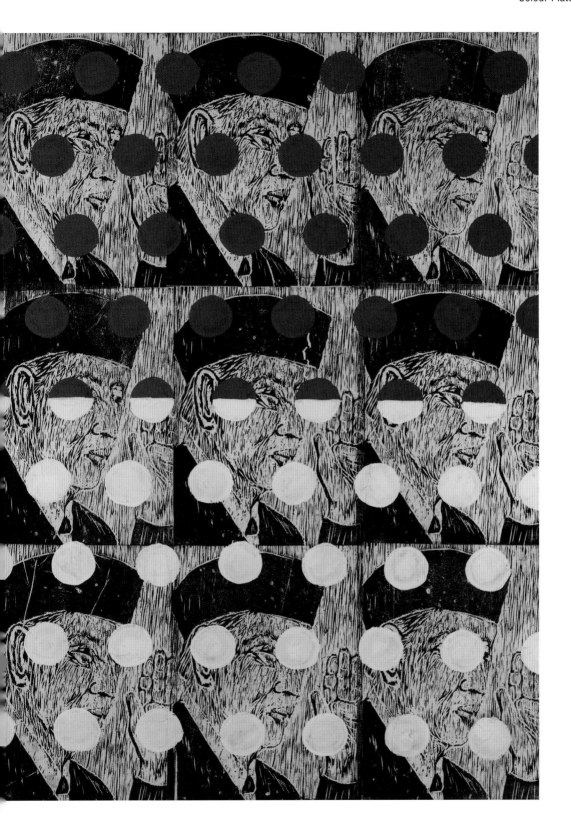

Portrait and Veil, 2009, oil on canvas, 100 x 80 cm, artist collection

Salam, 2009, oil on canvas, 100 x 80 cm, artist collection

White Cloud, 2009, oil on canvas, 120 x 100 cm, artist collection

Curriculum Vitae

Website www.vincentleow.com
Date of Birth 7 December 1961

SELECTED SOLO EXHIBITIONS

2010 8Q, Singapore Art Museum
"Tags and Treats" paintings and sculpture

2009 SooBin Art In'l, Singapore "Black Gold"
printmaking, woodcut

2007 Xin Beijing Gallery, Beijing, China.
"Andy's Pranks and Swimming Lessons"
paintings and sculptures

2004 Jendala Visual Art Space @ Esplande, Singapore
"Mock Ducks and Manicured Poodles" paintings

2001 TADU Art Space, Bangkok, Thailand
"Four Eyes, Cloudy Skies", paintings

2000 LIP Gallery, Yogyakarta, Indonesia.
"Caged Feet", installation

1998 TK Studios Gallery, Singapore
"Mountian Cow Milk Factory", sculpture installation

1996 Substation Gallery, Singapore
"Falling Bones, Hungry Chillies", paintings

1994 Substation Gallery, Singapore
"Chop Suey", paintings

1992 Shenn's Gallery, Singapore "Donkeys, Elephants
& The Three Legged Toad", paintings

1991 School 33 Art Centre, Maryland, USA
"Vincent Leow: Recent Paintings"

SELECTED GROUP EXHIBITIONS

2009 "Thirst IV" group exhibition, Sharjah Art Museum,
Sharjah, UAE

2008 "Royal Academy of Arts Summer Exhibition",
London, UK
"Peace Postcard Exhibition" UNESCO, Sharjah, UAE
"THIRST III" group exhibition, REWARK Gallery,
Sharjah, UAE

2007 "Domesticity" Seoul Museum of Art, Seoul, Korea.
52nd Venice Biennale of Contemporary Art,
Singapore Pavilion, Italy
3rd GuiYang Biennale of Contemporary Art,
Guiyang, China

2005 "World Expo 2005 Singapore pavilion,
Nagoya, Japan
"Contemporary Self-Portraiture/Reassessing
Identity, ICAS, Singapore

2004 "11th Asian Art Biennale" Osmani Memorial Hall,
Bangladesh

2003 "RENGA Paintings" National Art Gallery,
Kuala Lumpur, Malaysia

2002 "P.A.U.S.E" Gwanju Biennale 2002, Korea
"Nokia Singapore Art" Singapore Art Museum,
Singapore

2000 "ParallelWorld" Project 304 Bangkok, Thailand
"Feast" group exhibition, Singapore Art Museum,
Singapore

1999 "Provocative Things" Sculpture Square, Singapore
"Art et Politique", Sarcelles, France

1998 "Bangkok Art Project", Bangkok
"Second Nature: Cityscapes of Singapore",
Central Plaza, Hong Kong
"Imagining Self", Singapore Art Museum, Singapore

1997 "9th Indian Triennial of Contemporary Art",
New Delhi, India

1996 "Shell Grand Discovery Art Exhibition", Singapore
"TOUR de ART LAH !" Singapore Festival of the Arts,
Singapore.

1995 "Chiang Mai Social Installation", Chiang Mai,
Thailand
"Fighting the Universal Spider", A & O Gallery, Berlin,
Germany
"A Flog of Birdies" Black Box, TheatreWorks,
Singapore

1994 "Para Values" Site specific installation, Fort Canning
Park, Singapore
"Window on Singapore Art" China & Hong Kong,
Singapore

1993 "International Sculpture & Painting Symposium",
Gulbarga, India
"5th Fukui International Biennial", Tawara,
Fukui City, Japan
"1st Asia Pacific Triennial of Contemporary Art",
Brisbane, Australia

1992 "Performance Art Week", Gallery 21, Singapore
"HOPE" Visual Art Exhibition, 5th Passage, Singapore

1991 "Many in One: Art From Singapore",
Washington DC, USA
"Vincent Leow & Rudy Nadler", Maryland Institute,
Baltimore, USA
"Urban Artists in Singapore" National Museum
Art Gallery, Singapore

1990 "ARTSCAPE 90", Decker Gallery, Baltimore, USA
"EYE 21" ART Base Gallery, Singapore

1989 "The Drawing Show" Artists Village, Singapore
"QU ArtSupport II" QU Art Space, Hong Kong
"Contemporary Art in Singapore ", Netherlands
& Germany
"Two with a Cause", National Art Gallery, Singapore

1988 "The Artists Village Show" open studio show, Artists
Village, Singapore "7th Discovery Arts Exhibition",
Shell Tower, Singapore

1987 "National Museum Centenary Exhibition", Singapore

1986 "Australian Art Award for Young Artists", National
Museum, Singapore
"3rd Sculpture Workshop & Exhibition" LASELLE
College of Arts, Singapore

1985 "3rd ASEAN Young Painting Workshop & Exhibition",
Indonesia
"2nd Sculpture Workshop & Exhibition", National Art
Gallery, Singapore

AWARDS

2002 Japanese Chamber of Commerce and Industry, Singapore
- JCCI Culture Award

2000 UNESCO-ASCHBERG
- Artists in Residence, Yogyakarta, Indonesia

1991 Maryland Institute College of Art, Baltimore, USA
- Mount Royal Scholarship

1990 Lee Foundation, Singapore
- Overseas Scholarship Bursary
Singapore Cultural and Community Arts Grant (NAC), Singapore
- Overseas Bursary
Maryland Institute College of Art, Baltimore, USA
- Mount Royal Scholarship

1989 Lee Foundation, Singapore
- Overseas Scholarship Bursary
Singapore Cultural and Community Arts Grant (NAC), Singapore
- Overseas Bursary

1988 Lee Foundation, Singapore
- Exhibition Grant

1987 Sentosa Sculpture Design Competition, Singapore
- First prize award

ART PROJECTS & COMMISSIONS

2009 Abu Dhabi Tourism Board
- ART CAR (painting)

2007 Draycott Park Condominium, Singapore.
- Friendship Pups, public art (stainless sculpture)

1999 Kranji Turf Club, Singapore
- Red Numbers, public art (aluminum sculpture)

1999 –2001 Land Transport Authority, Singapore.
- Northeast line MRT mural, Lorong Buangkok Station, public art

1996 Sentosa, Singapore
- Water Feature at Merlion Walk, public art (water feature in Mosiac)

1996 Singapore Technologies
- "OPEL VECTRA ART CAR" public art (painting)

1990 National Museum Art Gallery, Singapore
- "DREAM WORLD" video Installation
Singapore Festival of Arts, Singapore
- "Their Piece" interactive sculpture project

1989 Katong Convent Secondary School, Singapore
- "Love & Peace" public art (cement fondu sculpture)

1987 Sentosa Development Corporation, Singapore
- "Beach Fun" public art (cement fondu sculpture)

COLLECTIONS

- Singapore Art Museum: paintings, sculptures and installation
- Deutsche Bank Singapore: works on paper
- National Arts Council: a series of silk screen print on paper
- National Institute of Education: painting
- Fukuoka Art Museum: mixed medium work on paper
- Private Collections: paintings, sculptures, prints and drawing

HIGHER EDUCATION

2005 Doctor of Fine Art,
RMIT University, Melbourne, Australia

QUALIFICATION

1991 Master of Fine Art,
Maryland Institute College of Art, Baltimore, USA

1987 Diploma in Fine Art, Sculpture (Merit Award),
LASALLE College of the Arts, Singapore

CURRENT POSITION

Associate Professor, Painting Fine Art, Programme Chair
College of Fine Art and Design, University of Sharjah

EMPLOYMENT HISTORY

2003–2007 LASALLE-SIA College of the Arts, Singapore
Senior Lecturer, Fine Arts Post-Graduate Studies

1997–1999 National University of Singapore, Architecture
Part-time Lecturer to Year 1 Architectural students

1998–2003 Plastique Kinetic Worms, Visual Art Space,
Singapore Artistic Director

1995–1997 Lycée Français de Singapour
Adjunct Art teacher to Secondary 1,2,3,4 students

1993–1995 LASALLE-SIA College of the Arts, Singapore
Lecturer, Head of Sculpture Department,
Diploma in Fine Art

PUBLIC AND PROFESSIONAL SERVICE / MEMBERSHIP / COMMITTEE

2007– University of Sharjah, College of Fine Art and Design Programme Development and Accreditation Committee (Fine Arts)
Faculty Promotion Committee member

2004–2007 LASALLE-SIA College of the Arts, Singapore
Research Review Committee member

2000 Singapore Art Museum
Public Sculpture Review Committee member

1997– Plastique Kinetic Worms, President and Committee Member

1996–2006 National Arts Council, Singapore
Visual Art Resource Panel Member

Bibliography

Exhibition Catalogue Publications

"Caged Feet" Exhibition Catalogue, Cemeti Art Foundation, Yogyakarta, Indonesia, 2000.

Kunavichyanont, Sutee, "Bangkok Art Project" Exhibition Catalogue, Bangkok, Thailand, 1998.

Kwok, Kian Chow, "Channels and Confluences: A History on Singapore Art", Singapore Art Museum Publication, 1996.

Lee, Joanna, "9th Indian Triennial of Contemporary Art" Exhibition Catalogue, India, 1997.

Lim, Karen, "CRISP", Singapore Art Museum Publication, 1999.

Nadarajan, Gunalan, "Ambulation" Exhibition Catalogue, Earl Lu Gallery, 1998.

O'Neil, Mathieu, "Mixage" Exhibition Catalogue, Alliance Française, Singapore, 1999.

Poh, Lindy, Ray Lagenbach, Wee Wan Ling, Pwee Keng Hock, "Four Eyes Cloudy Skies" Exhibition Catalogue, Atelier Frank and Lee, Tadu Contemporary Art Space, Bangkok, Thailand, 2001.

Poh, Lindy & T.K. Sabapathy, "Andy Pranks and Swimming Lessons" Exhibition Catalogue, Xin Beijing Gallery, Soobin International, 2007.

Poh, Lindy & T.K. Sabapathy, "Mock Ducks and Manicured Poodles" Exhibition Catalogue, Jendela Visual Art Space @ the Esplanade, Singapore, 2004.

Poshyananda, Apinan, "Body Language", Scrap Books, 1995.

Sabapathy, T.K., "1st Asia Pacific Triennial of Contemporary Art", Exhibition Catalogue, Queensland Art Gallery, Brisbane, 1993.

Sabapathy, T.K., "Provocative Things", Exhibition Catalogue, Sculpture Square, Singapore, 1999.

Wong, Susie, "Vincent Leow", South East Asian Art Today, Roeder Publication, Singapore, 1996.

Newspaper and Magazine Reviews

"Student's 'Beach Fun' Sculpture Tops Sentosa Design Contest", The Straits Times, 18 Jul 1987.

Ang, Dave, "Revolting", The New Paper, 9 Feb 1993.

Chan Hsia Siang, "Beach Fun", Sin Ming Daily, 17 Jul 1985.

Chengzu, "Mediator on Canvas", Bangkok Post, 21 Jun 2001.

Chew, David, "Setting Style Overtime", Venice Biennale, iSh Magazine, 2007.

Chew, David, "V Days, Singapore gets Fantastical in Venice", Today, Feb 2007.

Chia, Adeline, "Venice Calling", The Straits Times, 26 Apr 2007.

Chia Ming Chien, "Heart on Art", MAN Life and Style Magazine, Jun/Jul 1988.

Chong, June, "Biennale Art Piece Veiled", The Straits Times, 24 May 2007.

Chong, June, "Four to Show at Venice Biennale", The Straits Times, 1 Feb 2007.

Chong, June, "Venetian Inspiration", The Straits Times, 15 Sep 2007.

Chow, Clara, "Buy a Bit of Buangkok", The Straits Times, 16 Nov 2005.

Chow, Clara, "Reality vs Fiction", The Straits Times, 12 Aug 2004.

Farnay, Rachel, "Vincent Leow at The Substation", Asian Art News, Nov/Dec 1996.

Finlay, Victoria, "Brushing Off a Boring Image", The Review Arts, Hong Kong, 10 Oct 1998.

Goh K.K., "Chop Suey", Lianhe Zaobao, 14 May 1994.

Goh K.K., "Donkeys, Elephants and the Three-Legged Toad", *Lianhe Zaobao*, 17 Oct 1992.

Goh K.K., "Four Eyes, Cloudy Skies", *Lianhe Zaobao*, 21 Apr 2001.

Goh K.K., "Mock Ducks and Manicured Poodles", *Lianhe Zaobao*, 30 Aug 2004.

Goh K.K., "Ren Nian Guo", *Lianhe Zaobao*, 11 Sep 2007.

Harper, Glenn, "Volume and Form", *Sculpture Magazine*, Sep 1999.

Ho Tzu Nyen, "Vincent Leow: Mock Ducks & Manicured Poodles", *Art Asia Pacific*, Winter Issue, No. 43, Pg. 77, 2005.

Jacobson, Howard, "Peanut Get Monkey", *Modern Painters*, Oct 1998.

Farney, Rachel, "Eyes Wide Open", *The Arts Magazine*, 2001.

Farney, Rachel, "Renewal Paintings", *The Arts Magazine*, 2001.

Jay Sian E., "Facing Up to Artistic Space", *The Straits Times*, 2 Nov 1999.

Koh Buck Song, "But Is It Art", *The Straits Times*, 29 Nov 1991.

Lau Siew Mei, "Rage and Loathing at Artists' Show", *The Straits Times*, 1 Jun 1989.

Lee, Vanessa, "A Mix of Nightmarish Objects and Relaxing Prints", *Business Times*, 13 Jun 1988.

Lee Weng Choy, "New Criteria: Rearticulating the Other", *Art Asia Pacific*, Vol. 3, No. 1, 1996.

Lee Weng Choy, "The Public Cows of Vincent Leow", *Eyeline Magazine*, Spring 1998.

Low Sze Wee, "Go Ahead, Stomp on the Art", *The Straits Times*, 1998.

Lui, John, "Take Some Scrap Parts, Use Your Imagination and Get Your Sculpture", *The Sunday Times*, 20 Jun 1993.

Mun Y-Jean, "Mock, Manicured and Kinetic", *The Peak*, Vol. 21, Issue 8, pg. 131, Aug 2005.

Nayar, Parvathi, "Vincent Leow Goes to Venice Biennale", *Business Times*, 2 Feb 2007.

Ni, Fred, "USA? Hot Dog! Vincent Leow's Donkeys, Elephants and the 3 Legged Toad Show", *8 Days* magazine, Oct 1992.

Oon, Clarrissa, "S'pore Artists Pick Mixed Media for Asian Show", *The Straits Times*, 9 Jan 2004.

Richard, Paul, "Generic Singapore", *The Washington Post*, 13 Jun 1991.

Sabapathy, T.K., "A Stimulating Show of Energy and Humor", *The Straits Times*, 16 May 1994.

Sabapathy, T.K., "Animal Attractions", *The Straits Times*, 15 Oct 1992.

Sabapathy, T.K., "Artists' Colony in Ulu Sembawang", *The Straits Times*, 1988.

Sabapathy, T.K., "Magic, Mystery and a Hint of Danger", *The Straits Times*, 17 Jul 1989.

Sasitharan, T., "Definitely Not a Show of Pretty Paintings", *The Straits Times*, 11 Jul 1989.

Sasitharan, T., "On the Path to Discover", *The Straits Times*, 1988.

See Swee Hsia, "ASEAN Youth Painting Workshop", *Lianhe Wanbao*, 1 Dec 1985.

Szep, Jason, "Singapore in Awkward Embrace with Arts", *Reuters*, Oct 2004.

Wood, Carol, "Show & Tell", *City Paper*, Baltimore, MD, USA, Jan 1992.

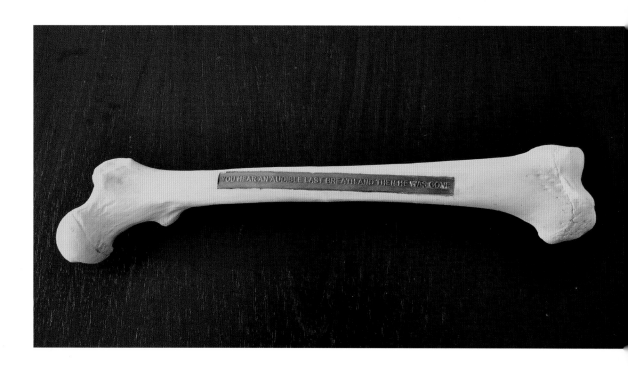